On Generosity

A Way Forward in a Divided World

JOHN LEE

STONE TOWER PRESS

On Generosity

Stone Tower Press
7 Ellen Rd.
Middletown, RI 02842
stonetowerpress.com

ISBN: 978-1-7368651-9-4

Cover design and text formatting by Amy Cole and Amy Landheer of JPL Design Solutions

Front cover illustration is *The Starry Night* by Vincent van Gogh.

Printed in the United States of America
First printing

Contents

Acknowledgments

Acknowledging people is one of the most gratifying parts of a project. It underlines that no one does anything alone. First, I thank Tim Demy, who read through the manuscript and made helpful suggestions, especially in terms of readability. I also thank him for his patience and flexibility, which this project needed. I also thank Daniel Park, Sam Kim, and Joanne Lu for reading an early draft of the book. They gave sage advice and helped me shape it. I added chapter six because of their comments. James Lee read a revised draft and offered needed encouragement. A word of thanks also goes to Fred Kim, who asked me to offer a rationale for looking at the New Testament as a text for generosity. Ben Spalink and Peter Armstrong read the penultimate draft and saved me from several blunders. Finally, Susie Case finetuned a few chapters with her discerning eye.

A special word of thanks goes to my former, current, and partner congregations that allowed me to share these ideas this season—Good News, City Grace, and Newtown. Finally, I also thank my family who embodies generosity. My parents have given with open hands and hearts. I first saw what generosity looks like through them; in fact, they naturalized it.

About the Cover

A copy of Van Gogh's painting *Starry Night* has been hanging on the wall of my son's bedroom since he was a little boy. My wife introduced a book of paintings to him when he was an infant, and a few of Van Gogh's works were in the collection. Quickly, *Starry Night* became his favorite. My son is now in college, and I use his room as a study during most of the year. From time to time, I gaze upon the painting, and I see generosity. There is an abundance of stars, and I think of God's promise to Abraham in Genesis 15:5 declaring that his descendants will be as the stars of the sky. And on the upper righthand corner, an amalgamation of the moon and sun floats and casts a soft glow. It is benevolent.

The painting is of a French city, Arles. But the interesting point is that there is a Dutch Reformed church in the center. It looks like the Dutch Reformed church I attend, which has been standing for nearly 300 years, predating Van Gogh.

All is peaceful in Arles and divine beneficence swirls around. I imagine families around a wooden table passing bread, playing board games, and enjoying the company of loved ones. I hear laughter and the giggling of children at their uncle's antics. I can almost smell the pastries and gustatory delights of French desserts. The yellow marks of paint on the windows suggest the warmth of familial life. There is one building, however, whose lights are conspicuously off—the church in the center of the city. The whiteness of the church makes the darkness darker. I don't know if Van Gogh is making a statement about the church of his day. He lived during the time of Abraham Kuyper and Herman Bavinck, but he died before he saw the fruits of their labor. At the church's best, I see a different painting. The lights are on, and it sways with the divine swirls. God is generous; we only need to look around.

Introduction

The idea for this short book unfolded in the winter months of 2021 as the world around me seemed to be tearing at the seams. Racial tension was high, anti-Asian sentiment was rising, and the wealth gap was staggering, not to mention a second surge of the coronavirus was underway. As I write, Jeff Bezos has a net worth of over $200 billion. Enough said.

I sat at my local coffee shop, thinking that my children would inherit a world more polarized and intolerant than the one in which I was raised. My childhood was not idyllic or innocent. Racism was explicit, students were jumped on their way to school, including myself, and gangs were on the rise. Yet, all that seems quaint compared to what we are now witnessing.

As a Christian, I thought a theology of generosity was an essential part of the solution. No matter what answers people come up with—political, social, or economic—generosity must fill it, better yet saturate it because we live in a diverse world with conflicting interests, which breeds mistrust and even hatred. In such a context, a generous spirit is better than an indifferent one and far better than one that is miserly.

Most would agree that the polarization we see is a cause for concern, and the trends are not promising. Ezra Klein, a columnist for the New York Times, writes:

> We are so locked into our political identities that there is virtually no candidate, no information, no condition, that can force us to change our minds. We will justify almost anything or anyone so long as it helps our side, and the result is a politics devoid of guardrails, standards, persuasion, or accountability.[1]

A new tribalism is here where people flock to those who share the same opinions. And they simply cannot believe that others can't see what they see. According to Jonathan Haidt, a professor at New York University, "America's hyperpartisanship is now a threat to the world."[2] When we add social media into the calculus with its customization of algorithms that appeal to a person's tastes, information is curated, biases are confirmed, and convictions become calcified. Once again Klein writes: "That algorithm isn't just an engine of radicalization; it's an engine of identity."[3] Once our views become our identity, change becomes difficult, and generosity toward other people withers and animosity begins.

Concerning the connection between animosity and identity, few have written as penetratingly and powerfully as Amin Maalouf, a Lebanese-born French author. He offers a stern warning from his own experience. He writes:

> People often see themselves in terms of whichever one of these allegiances is most under attack. And sometimes, when a person doesn't have the strength to defend that allegiance, he hides it. Then it remains buried deep down in the dark, awaiting revenge. But whether he accepts or conceals it, proclaims it discreetly or flaunts it, it is with allegiance that the person concerned identifies. And then, whether it relates to colour, religion, language or class, it invades the person's whole identity.[4]

Are we getting to the point in our country where identity politics is creating a deep well of hatred awaiting revenge? I think so.

This book does not seek to offer a grand strategy. Its purpose is to urge people toward generosity—those on the right, the left, and in between. Generosity requires open hearts, and hearts that are open are disarming. Moreover, when people are disarmed, they can embrace each other.

The best literature on generosity is the New Testament. There is broad agreement among scholars that Christianity was the catalyst behind charity to the poor and the marginalized. In other words, a new type of generosity emerged with Christianity where generosity was extended to people who could not reciprocate. Paul Veyne, the great French historian, states: "The triumph of the Christian religion enabled a strong minority to make an entire society sensitive to poverty…Alms were to be given in obedience to God's commandment."[5] In the same paragraph, he matter-of-factly continues: "The consequences of this triumph were very marked. Paganism had abandoned without much remorse the starving, the old, and the sick. Old people's homes, orphanages, hospitals and so on are institutions that appear only with the Christian epoch, the very names for them being neologisms in Latin and Greek."[6] Two of the greatest historians of this period confirm this picture—Henry Chadwick and Peter Brown.[7] N. T. Wright, arguably the greatest living New Testament scholar, concurs.[8] The ancient sources also agree.[9] And Rodney Stark, a sociologist of religion, comes to similar conclusions.[10]

What sits behind Christian charity is the New Testament. Hence, this book is a meditation on generosity in the ministry of the apostle Paul. In a very real way, Paul changed the world through generosity, a point that is easily forgotten in view of his profound pen. He was the apostle of inclusion with his Gentile mission. He was a pluralist before the word was in fashion. He also loved the poor. Even in a second century apocryphal text, *The Acts of Paul and Thecla,* he is portrayed as a champion of the poor—such is his legacy.[11]

Techniques, strategies, demographic studies, and the like too often fill the church's mind and heart, but rarely will these data points move people. In addition, much of the so-called insights of the social sciences are flimsy, a point that Alasdair MacIntyre and Neil Postman humorously point out with devilish delight.[12] Generosity, on the other hand, changes people, moves them, and transforms them. From this perspective, the New Testament offers a better way—fewer statistics, less techniques, more examples of generosity, and most of all, a theology of generosity that is as deep as it is wide and high. My hope is that we will consider its vision and allow it to shape our hearts. Those outside the Christian tradition may want to view this book as a curious visitor peering in to see the workings of faith and its implications. They may don the hat of an anthropologist and consider its message from a safe distance.

Originally, these essays (except for chapter six) started as sermons, preached at The Reformed Church of Newtown in Elmhurst, Queens, during the pandemic that swept around the world. Elmhurst was particularly hit hard, as it became the epicenter of the first wave of the pandemic in America. To honor this courageous and extraordinary congregation, I've kept some of the homiletic elements intact. If at times, the prose sounds sermonic, you know why. The sixth essay is a sketch of Paul's testimony of sacrifice. It seemed proper to examine the person and not just his pen. The final essay touches a related theme, imagination. I decided to add it because we must reimagine the world with a heart of generosity and break through the narratives that those in power spin. Our imaginations are one of the most powerful gifts that God has given. Finally, though the essays are united in theme, they do not need to be read in order. Each stands alone.

I dedicate this book to four people whose heart of generosity blessed my life: Matthew Choi, Brian Chang, Christine Marocco, and Lester Lin. My prayer is that generosity will flow outward. If it does, the beauty of it will change the world.

ENDNOTES

1. Klein, *Why We're Divided,* xiv.
2. Haidt, *The Righteous Mind,* 321.
3. Klein, *Why We're Divided,* 157.
4. Maalouf, *In the Name of Identity,* 26. Maalouf's book is an insightful exploration of identity.
5. Veyne, *Bread and Circuses,* 33.
6. Veyne, *Bread and Circuses,* 33. Veyne is fully aware that the ancient world was generous, but that generosity only extended to those that could give something in return. He writes: "There was no finer virtue than to be open-handed, or, as they said in those days, to have a great soul—provided that the recipient himself or itself was also great: not a slave, a poor wretch, some unknown allies." Veyne, *Bread and Circuses,* 101. Tarn, the great Hellenistic historian, writes: "Yet amid all the philanthropic feeling and public spirit of the time, philanthropy in our sense—the organized aid of the poor by the rich—was almost unknown. Broadly speaking, pity for the poor had little place in the normal Greek character..." W. W. Tarn, *Hellenistic Civilization,* 110.
7. "The practical application of charity was probably the most potent single cause of Christian success." Chadwick, *The Early Church,* 56. "To put it bluntly; in a sense, it was the Christian bishops who invented the poor. They rose to leadership in late Roman society by bringing the poor into ever-sharper focus. Brown, *Poverty and Leadership,* 8.
8. "By the end of second century, Roman officials were not particularly aware of the nuances of Christian teachings, but they did know what the word 'bishop' meant—it meant someone who kept on agitating about the needs of the poor. And at point after

point, these strands of community life went back to Paul. He had planted these seeds." N. T. Wright, *Paul—A Biography*, 427.

9. Julian, *Ep.* 22.430D; Arist., *Apol.* 15; Tert., *Apol.* 39.

10. See Rodney Stark's *The Rise of Christianity.* We can also add Wayne Meeks, a great historian of early Christianity. "...it can hardly be doubted that the Christian family of moral sensibilities has profoundly affected the history of morality, most clearly in European culture and its diasporas, but also to some extent in every part of the modern world." Meeks, *The Origins of Christian Morality*, 3.

11. Elliot, *The Apocryphal New Testament.* 364-388.

12. MacIntyre, *After Virtue*, 88-108; Postman, *Technopoloy*, 44-163.

"We want you to know, brothers, about the grace of God that has been given among the churches of Macedonia, for in a severe test of affliction, their abundance of joy and their extreme poverty have overflowed in a wealth of generosity on their part. For they gave according to their means, as I can testify, and beyond their means, of their own accord, begging us earnestly for the favor of taking part in the relief of the saints—and this, not as we expected, but they gave themselves first to the Lord and then by the will of God to us. Accordingly, we urged Titus that as he had started, so he should complete among you this act of grace. But as you excel in everything—in faith, in speech, in knowledge, in all earnestness, and in our love for you—see that you excel in this act of grace also. I say this not as a command, but to prove by the earnestness of others that your love also is genuine. For you know the grace of our Lord Jesus Christ, that though he was rich, yet for your sake he became poor, so that you by his poverty might become rich. And in this matter I give my judgment: this benefits you, who a year ago started not only to do this work but also to desire to do it. So now finish doing it as well, so that your readiness in desiring it may be matched by your completing it out of what you have."

2 Corinthians 8:1-11

1

Generative Giving

Cicadas sing. Their sound is created by their corrugated exoskeletal structure, which is called a tymbal. Because they are partially hollow inside, when they vibrate their muscles, they produce music. Male cicadas do the singing in order to attract females. Sometimes, a group of male cicadas congregates and forms a chorus to attract more females. It works, and mating begins. Once eggs are fertilized, a female cicada cuts the bark of a twig and lays her eggs in it. When the eggs hatch, the nymphs fall to the ground, and they burrow eight feet into the earth. They live most of their lives underground. Some cicadas stay underground for 3 years, others for 13, still others for 17. When they finally emerge, they shed their skins and become the adult cicadas that we know, see, and hear. The 17-year cicada (Brood X) will emerge in 2021, this spring. This swarm of cicadas is making their ascent now. Soon we will hear the singing of cicadas in the Northeast.[1]

I bring up cicadas because they show us that cycles are built into nature. In this case, the cycle consists of singing, mating, laying eggs, burrowing, exiting, and back to singing. It happens every 17 years. Amazing, intricate, and beautiful. At this point, I would be remiss if I did not mention that some cycles are hellish, especially when violence and oppression are involved. The person who reflected on this topic more than most in recent history is Miroslav Volf.

In his book *Exclusion and Embrace,* Volf shows that violence too often begets more violence. He recounts the story of a teacher in the former Yugoslavia. When religious conflict broke out, Serbian soldiers attacked the Muslim population. In one school, a Muslim woman, a teacher of literature, was not only mocked but nearly beaten to death by her colleagues. In her battered and bruised state, a student whom she taught urinated in her mouth. This woman lost the ability to forgive that day as her hatred seethed. When she gave birth to her second child, she named him Jihad. As she suckled him, she said: "May this milk choke you if you forget."[2] Her anger is palpable, justifiable, and understandable, but if we look at her stance from another perspective, she is furthering a cycle, which not only encompasses her life but also her son's.

Volf's next point is provocative. Victims need to repent as well as perpetrators because victims often mimic the behavior of their oppressors and let themselves be shaped into their mirror image. He also notes that this hatred can intensify. He writes: "If victims do not repent today, they will become perpetrators tomorrow who, in their self-deceit, will seek to exculpate their misdeeds on account of their own victimization."[3] Some might accuse Volf of exaggerating, but the dynamic he describes is ubiquitous. Two years ago, a video of a South Korean man beating a Japanese woman went viral.[4] The cause for the attack was Japan's annexation of Korea in 1910. Something that took place over a century ago with little bearing on this man inflamed him to attack. Cycles linger.

Here is the point. Because life is filled with cycles, it behooves us to break bad ones that bring pain and start good ones that burst into life and bless people. And because cycles are generative, perpetual blessing can be the outcome—season after season. Sowing generously in the lives of people is one of the most beautiful cycles to begin. Paul makes this point into a principle in 2 Corinthians 9:6 when he writes: "The point is this: whoever sows sparingly will also reap sparingly, and whoever sows bountifully will also reap bountifully." He reminds the Corinthians of a paradoxical truth—spiritual blessing accumulates, accelerates, and grows when people give, not when they save.

Paul wants the Corinthians to know about the amazing cycle that the Macedonian churches started. Macedonian congregations swelled in rich generosity and created a cycle of giving. Paul's language is noteworthy because it shows that these groups created a good cycle amid incredible hardships. He says that the poverty of the Macedonians was one of depth. He squeezes a prepositional phrase, "down to the depth," between the article and the word it modifies, "poverty." Paul, therefore, is not speaking of an ordinary kind of poverty but a profoundly deep one.[5] It is important to pause here and reflect because the destitution that we see in our cities is not the same as the one in the ancient world. The great Roman historian, Ramsey MacMullen, offers a picture of ancient poverty when he writes:

> Nothing was wasted in the ancient world: not an abandoned baby, not the cloth that kept the ragpicker in business, not the empty fisherman's shack on the beach, not even the grain of barley in the horse manure on the streets. There were always people poor enough to fight over another's leavings.[6]

Can you picture what deep poverty looked like in the ancient world? Can you smell the manure, and a little girl picking a barley seed from it? A well-known rabbi, Johanan b. Zakkai, was walking the streets of Jerusalem and saw a young girl from a wealthy family reduced to nothing. She was the one picking a barley seed from the horse manure. He asked her what happened, and she said that her family lost everything in the war.[7] Unless we understand the logic and desperation of this story, it will be difficult to see how brutal life could be in the ancient world.

Paul also mentions trials.[8] He does not delve into what these trials were, but if we take the church of Philippi as representative (a leading city in Macedonia), then external challenges were mounting. False teachers were leading people astray and adversaries were intimidating the fledgling church. Concerning false teachers, Paul calls them dogs, evil doers, and mutilators of the flesh.[9] Their aim was self-aggrandizement at the expense of others.[10] Concerning external pressures, we do not know if persecution broke out, but the language Paul uses suggests that suffering was real. He writes:

> ...[do not be frightened] in anything by your opponents. This is a clear sign to them of their destruction, but of your salvation, and that from God. For it has been granted to you that for the sake of Christ you should not only believe in him but also suffer for his sake, engaged in the same conflict that you saw I had and now hear that I still have.[11]

The word he uses for opponents, *antikeimenoi*, slants towards mob violence. Paul uses the same word in 1 Corinthians 16:9 to refer to his troubles in Ephesus where mob violence exploded.[12] Moreover, Paul experienced opposition in his Macedonian ministry right from the beginning. In Philippi he was beaten and imprisoned, and in Thessalonica a mob sought to kill him and followed him to Berea.[13]

Paul's language is worth pointing out again. He says that the Macedonians abounded in the riches of generosity. The word he uses for generosity, *haplotās*, has a meaning that includes sincerity.[14] By using that word, Paul emphasizes heart issues. The Macedonians wanted to give from the heart, and so they gave, irrespective of their circumstances. In fact, according to Paul, they pleaded to give beyond their ability and entirely on their own. I imagine Paul trying to dissuade their giving so that they can use their meager resources for their own families, but they would not have it. Giving captured their hearts and compelled them to be lavish. The Macedonians, therefore, show that generosity is not pegged to circumstances—as if abundance is a prerequisite to give and dearth a reason not to give—but it is pegged to willingness of heart. The power of the heart is underlined. More importantly, this passage shows that God's grace swells hearts to give even in affliction.

In one of the great ironies of the New Testament, the more poverty-stricken areas did more for the advancement of the kingdom of God than wealthier ones. We would think richer cities, such as Corinth or Ephesus, would do something greater for God, but that picture would be inaccurate. The Corinthians were dysfunctional—theologically, socially, and spiritually. Often the cycles they created were self-serving. Think of their divisiveness, litigious culture, and classism that excluded many. And the Ephesians, by the time of the book of Revelation, were almost extinct because they lost their first love.[15] When God says that he works through the weak and poor, the Macedonian churches are a case in point. They not only gave to the suffering believers in Judea but also launched Paul's missionary endeavors, and their partnership with him impacted the world in profound ways. It would not be an exaggeration to say that the Macedonian churches (particularly, the Philippians) provided the greatest impetus and encouragement for Paul's missionary journeys, which indelibly changed the world.

Herein lies the challenge for the Corinthians (and for us)—cultivating generosity does not come naturally; effort and follow through are important, especially as the initial desire to give flickers and fades. According to Paul, the Corinthians excelled in many areas (faith, speech, and knowledge); now they ought to cultivate the practice of giving. So, Paul sends Titus to encourage them to complete their initial desire. He is even more pronounced when he directly exhorts them: "So now finish doing it as well, so that your readiness in desiring it may be matched by your completing it out of what you have."[16]

Paul's emphasis falls on the importance of completing. Paul mentions the idea of completing the work of giving once in 2 Corinthians 8:6 and twice in 2 Corinthians 8:11. Paul knows that the Corinthians will only taste the fruits of generous giving and understand its spiritual logic when they give. More importantly, he knows that the fruit of a cycle can only be experienced when the cycle is completed (and often only after several iterations). To put it another way, a start, no matter how good and noble, is defective without the completion of it. So, Paul urges the Corinthians to make good on their original desire to give. What can they do? Where can they find the strength to follow through?

Paul gets to the heart of the Christian message and the motivation for giving when he reminds the Corinthians of what they already know, namely, the grace of Christ. However, Paul clothes the grace of Christ in economic tones. He reminds the Corinthians that he who was rich embraced poverty so that those who were poor might become rich. He invites them to see their poverty apart from Christ as well as their riches in him. He also offers a concrete picture of the compelling power of grace. It is the secret power behind Macedonian giving. Paul now wants the Corinthians to understand this grace as well. When they do, they, too, will share.

If we step into the work of Christ, the cycle of generosity is writ large. The incarnation of Christ is an emptying of glory, and his death on the cross is a profound act of impoverishment—both acts of sacrificial giving.[17] In addition, when we come to the penultimate word that Jesus uttered, the theme of completion comes to the fore. *Tetelestai*, "It is finished," is one of the most beautiful words in the New Testament, a word that matches Jesus's action of pushing out his final breath and bowing his head.[18] The cycle of generosity is complete. The work he came to do he finished, and from there flows blessing and life to the people of God, the Corinthians included. Those who experience this depth of grace cannot help but give. To put it another way, given people give. In time, they will see a glorious harvest. It might take 17 years of underground growth like cicadas to emerge, but it will. That is where faith comes in. We sow for the future, for our children, and for our children's children. By millions of daily generous acts—a kind word, a smile, a donation, a good deed, a silent prayer, a call, a visit, an act of faith—blessings grow and emerge. In time, like Brood X, we will see a brood of blessing break out because God does not forget seeds of generosity.

ENDNOTES

1. Jiménez, Jesus. "Billions (Yes, Billions) of Cicadas Soon to Emerge from Underground." *The New York Times*, March 28, 2021. https://www.nytimes.com/2021/03/28/us/cicada-brood-x.html.
2. Volf, *Exclusion and Embrace*, 111.
3. Volf, *Exclusion and Embrace*, 117.
4. "Korean man under probe for attacking Japanese woman in Seoul." *Korea Times*. (2019, August 25). https://www.koreatimes.co.kr/www/nation/2019/08/251_274485.html.
5. Murray Harris writes: "Another paradox expressed in this verse is, 'generosity in the midst of poverty.' In itself πτωχεία signifies 'great poverty.' But to emphasize that the Macedonians had reached 'the very depths of destitution,' Paul adds the remarkable qualification κατὰ βάθους, literally 'down to the depth,' referring not to 'ever-deeper poverty,' but 'poverty at the deepest,' 'rock-bottom poverty,' 'extreme/profound poverty.'" Harris, *2 Corinthians*, 562.
6. MacMullen, *Roman Social Relations*, 14.
7. Büchler, *The Economic Conditions of Judea After the Destruction of the Second Temple*, 22.
8. 2 Cor. 8:2. Paul also adds the adjective "much" to emphasize that the trials were significant.
9. Phil. 3:2.
10. Phil. 3:19.
11. Phil. 1:28-30.
12. O'Brien, *The Epistle to the Philippians*, 153. Also see: Thiselton, *The First Epistle to the Corinthians*, 1330.

13. Acts 16:16-17:15.

14. "ἁπλότης is an exclusively Pauline word (seven uses). On three occasions it refers to 'sincerity' or 'simplicity' of mind (2 Cor. 11:3) or heart (Eph. 6:5; Col. 3:22), a simple-heartedness that prompts action that is full of integrity and not duplicitous." Harris, *2 Corinthians*, 562.

15. Rev. 2:4-6.

16. 2 Cor. 8:11.

17. Phil. 2:7-8.

18. John 19:30.

"I say this not as a command, but to prove by the earnestness of others that your love also is genuine. For you know the grace of our Lord Jesus Christ, that though he was rich, yet for your sake he became poor, so that you by his poverty might become rich. And in this matter I give my judgment: this benefits you, who a year ago started not only to do this work but also to desire to do it. So now finish doing it as well, so that your readiness in desiring it may be matched by your completing it out of what you have. For if the readiness is there, it is acceptable according to what a person has, not according to what he does not have. For I do not mean that others should be eased and you burdened, but that as a matter of fairness your abundance at the present time should supply their need, so that their abundance may supply your need, that there may be fairness. As it is written, 'Whoever gathered much had nothing left over, and whoever gathered little had no lack.'"

2 Corinthians 8:8-15

2

The Myopia of a Meritocracy

Most young Americans will agree that the default way of viewing the world is through a meritocratic lens. One poll shows that 77% of Americans believe in the connection between hard work and success. Other countries are not so optimistic. For example, only half of Germans believe hard work brings success.[1] The majority in Japan and France do not see a connection at all.[2] If we cast our eyes to the ancient world, then most see only the futility of work. Bruce Longenecker, a professor of Christian Origins at Baylor University, points out: "the myth of Sisyphus spoke of the futility of human existence for those who expected there to be some correlation between the amount of effort one mustered and one's consequent achievement."[3]

Today many people praise a meritocracy because it bypasses nepotism, old boy networks, and any sort of cronyism. To see it alive, just ask students who received admission to a top university. They will say that they worked diligently to earn a spot, and work they did. They might not say it that bluntly (that would be crass), but the feeling lurks. Michael Sandel, a political science professor at Harvard, states: "The years of strenuous effort demanded of applicants to elite universities almost forces them to believe that their success is their own doing, and that if they fall short, they have no one to blame but themselves."[4] Ask parents, most will say that their children worked tirelessly. The implication is that they deserve admissions. Better yet, ask admissions officers; they will praise the hard work and diligence of their students. I went to my son's first university welcome ceremony online because of the pandemic. The words were predictable. "Congratulations! You were admitted to the most selective year in the school's history. All your hard work paid off."

It would be more honest if the school said something like this: "You are very fortunate to have a spot here, after all 35,000 people applied. You might be the best suited for this university, but we are not certain. How do you even measure people's aptitudes and achievements from a piece of paper? Some were admitted because of legacy, others were admitted because you could pay the tuition, still others were admitted because we need to raise our ranking, help our athletic programs, or fit a special need of the university. I know that you worked diligently but so did many others. The admissions process is broken—just between us. All that said, we welcome you and wish you the best."

Such words are truer to life. Consider three facts. First, you have little to do with your intelligence or gifts, the ostensible factors for admissions. You were born with them. So, if math comes easily, and you write gorgeous prose, and you have photographic memory, can you really take credit? You did not work for them; you have them as gifts. Second, what if you were born on the Tibetan plateau? College would not be in your future, even if you were a prodigy. You would probably live and die in the same community and never cultivate your intellectual gifts. In a word, there are many contingencies that you have no control over. So, can you really take credit for your accomplishments? Third, even if you were born with intellectual giftedness and into a good family in an advanced economy, so are millions of others. College admissions is a crapshoot, or if you are Christian, it is on account of God's grace, a point that Columbia University professor Andrew Delbanco wants his readers to rediscover. According to Delbanco, there once was a time when our great universities understood this point well. "...Our oldest colleges have abandoned the cardinal principle of the religion out of which they arose: the principle that no human being deserves anything based on his or her merit."[5] And what is true of college admissions is true of everything else.

About twenty years ago, I received a phone call from a congregant whose mother was diagnosed with a very rare disease. It was so rare that you can count on two hands the number of people who had it. He asked for prayer and asked if my wife, a medical resident, knew anything about the disease. She had no clue. Why should she? The disease is not covered in typical medical education, and she was in a different specialty. But she did the dutiful thing. She researched the disease and was able to give comfort. A week later, she was interviewing for a fellowship. A guest lecturer was present, and guess what? The professor asked about this very disease—blank faces, except for one young medical resident who happened to be applying for a fellowship to that very university hospital. The chair of the department was impressed when my wife, off the top of her head, spoke eloquently about the disease. When she interviewed, about an hour later, he practically offered her a spot. If you are an atheist, you would call this chance or good fortune. If you are a Christian, you would call it God's providence and favor. No one would call it merit.

In 1958, Michael Young, a politician and social scientist, penned a book, *The Rise of the Meritocracy*. It was prophetic because it depicts the sentiment of the modern world with uncanny precision. The book is in the form of an essay that chronicles the rise of a meritocracy in

England from World War II (which the book calls Hitler's War) to 2034. Competition in the sciences with other nations propelled a meritocratic view of life. Young depicts a world where intelligence and effort create a new caste of elites. Through science, intelligent children are discovered and honed to accomplish great things; others are left to do manual chores. Young does not say that society is divided into masters and slaves. He does not have to because he shows it. The intelligent deserve their good lives and the less intelligent deserve their common ones; one has merit, the other has nothing. To put it more sharply, the genetically superior deserve their wealth; the poor deserve their poverty. In one chapter, he states that five percent is the golden number, a brilliant class of people.[6] In another chapter, he says that about a third of all adults are useless because "the complexity of civilization had grown beyond them; owing to the lack of intelligence, they could not find niches."[7] The only thing they are capable of is serving others, a meritocratic serfdom. Young wrote the work to show that a consistent outworking of a meritocracy is highly undesirable. The modern irony is that Young's dystopia is becoming our vision of the good life.

Paul's interaction with the Corinthians shows one of the challenges to generosity, the hidden logic of merits. If we are going to make gains in generosity, then we need to focus our attention on the falsehoods of a meritocracy.

An understanding of grace levels a meritocratic edifice, no matter how intricately built. Paul's point is threefold. First, he aims for equality. Second, he tries to show that giving and receiving are paradoxical. Third, he reminds the Corinthians that God is the ultimate giver.

The main point of 2 Corinthians 8:8-15 is to argue for a kind of equality. We cannot press Paul's words to create an elaborate theology of equality, but what is certain is that those who have more should share with those who have less. In this context, Corinth, a relatively wealthy congregation, should share their resources with the struggling ones in Jerusalem. We see a picture of such giving in Acts 4, where several people sell their properties to support the fledgling church in need. It is in this context, we first read of Barnabas, whom the apostles call son of encouragement. The language of Acts 4 is similar to Paul's words in 2 Corinthians 8: "And with great power the apostles were giving their testimony to the resurrection of the Lord Jesus, and great grace was upon them all."[8] Grace so suffused the community that giving was the natural reflex. What is true then should be true now. Christians should be the most generous because they understand and have experienced grace. In other words, they have received lavishly what they did not work for or what they deserve. So, giving becomes the natural outflow.

Jesus's parable of the workers in the field reaches the

same conclusion. In it, all the workers receive the same wage whether they work the whole day, a part of the day, or a brief hour. When the time comes to pay the workers, those who were hired last are given a denarius. Those who worked longer (especially those who worked for twelve hours) believe that they should earn more even though they were hired to work for a denarius. After they receive their denarius, they complain: "These last worked only one hour, and you have made them equal to us who have borne the burden of the day and the scorching heat."[9] The owner of the field responds: "Am I not allowed to do what I choose with what belongs to me? Or do you begrudge my generosity?"[10] The laborers have merits in mind; the owner has fairness and generosity. When the parable ends, the narrative voice breaks in with the dictum that turns a meritocratic view upside-down: the last will be first, and the first last."[11] If we interpret this parable in the context of the first century, then the latecomers refer to tax collectors and sinners.[12] Grace and merits mix uneasily. Does this mean that Christians must take a vow of poverty and give everything away?

Paul makes it clear that he is not aiming for a kind of social revolution. He writes: "Our desire is not that others might be relieved while you are hard pressed, but that there might be equality."[13] The Corinthians do not need to impoverish themselves, but they should give generously.

What does this mean? Paul does not give guidelines, but there is a clue. The Corinthians should fulfill what they committed to give.[14] The assumption is that people should go before God, seek counsel as to their giving, and then give.

A. W. Tozer, a great twentieth-century American pastor, is helpful on this point. In a few of his writings, he makes the point that we can have many things, but we must not possess or own them.[15] Abraham, for example, was a rich man, but he learned not to possess his belongings. At one point, he gave up two sons.[16] Stewardship is underlined. God allows us to hold things for a season so that we can use them to manifest his love to others. Meister Eckhart, the medieval theologian, philosopher, and mystic, makes the same point in a more pointed way when he writes: "For all the gifts which [God] ever gave us, those both of nature and of grace, were given with the sole intention that we should possess nothing of our own…It is that he wishes to be our sole possession…"[17] This perspective changes everything because as we learn to possess nothing, we also learn that God is our possession. Hence, we are always rich and so giving becomes natural. And in the end, we step towards greater equality.

Second, giving is never one-sided. Seasons change. We might be in a position to give at one point, but a season of receiving might come. It is not inconceivable that one day the churches in Jerusalem will bless the Corinthians. History teaches us that fortunes change, sometimes radically. More importantly, when we view giving not only in terms of financial exchange, then giving and receiving take place all the time. For example, the Philippians might have given to Paul financially, but Paul sowed in them and others to the point where he could say that he carries about in his body the death of Christ.[18] And what they created was a beautiful and powerful partnership, which sowed in others. In fact, right in the beginning of Philippians, Paul praises God for the partnership (*koinonia*) that he has with them.[19] They gave to him, and he gave to them, and this partnership gave to the world.

There is also a more paradoxical giving and receiving that takes place. When mutual giving becomes the norm, everyone wins. The introduction to 1 John shows this point. John says that he is preaching the message of Christ to complete his joy.[20] We would expect him to say that he is sharing the message of Christ to complete the joy of his hearers.[21] That John does not say this shows that he is getting at something else, a paradoxical understanding of giving that is easy to miss. The one who gives is more blessed than the one who receives. And the reason for this is that in our giving we gain more of God.

I once interviewed a young woman for church

membership. I started in my customary way by asking her about her story. She told me that she was the daughter of a pastor. Her father served a megachurch in Seoul, Korea as an associate minister. She loved her life. I recall a small detail that was emblematic of her happy childhood. After a day at school and dinner with her parents, she would play the piano, and her father would sit next to her and listen, a beautiful picture of the bond between a father and daughter.

One day, her life changed. Her father and mother decided to become missionaries. Her perfect childhood was shattered in her mind. She moved to a remote area of the country where life was difficult—no running water, no amenities of a modern city, and most of all, no more undivided attention from her parents. Her mother and father thrust themselves into the lives of orphans. So, she had to share her parents with other children. This made her bitter towards God, and she became a nominal member of a church as an adult.

One day God began tugging at her heart. She decided to do something that she never thought she would. She went on a mission trip. She did not know what to expect, but she worked with orphans. On the last day, the children with tears streaming down their cheeks said their farewells. As she was pulling away in a taxi, her heart longed for them as much as they longed for her. They ran towards the taxi. She could see their faces in the mirror of the car with all their emotions and love. At that very moment, God whispered a question into her heart: "Do you now see why I called your father as a missionary?" All bitterness lifted, and she became a new person. She realized it was a privilege to share her father with children who had no one. Who received more? She would say that she did. When we give, we ultimately receive.

There is a third point. Paul refers to the Old Testament to buttress his argument. It is a near verbatim quote of Exodus 16:18 in the Septuagint (the early Greek translation of the Old Testament, also known as LXX). In that passage, Moses mentions God's miraculous provision. Every morning people went out and found thin flakes on the desert floor. They gathered them for that day. Some gathered much; others gathered less, but no one was in need. God in a very real sense gave them their daily bread. The point that God was teaching them was that he will provide for them.

In the New Testament, this bread from heaven is Christ. He shows it by multiplying the loaves and fish and by instituting the Lord's Supper. Even more importantly, his flesh becomes true bread on the cross.[22] In a word, he gives himself. There is no greater act of giving than the giving of yourself, and Jesus gives himself to us from his incarnation to his death and resurrection. This means that we are always recipients. So, when we give, we do so only because we have antecedently received.

Now how does all this tie in with merits? We have none. It is when we realize this humbling fact that paradoxically we free ourselves from ourselves, which leads to a society that seeks the common good. Michael Sandel makes this very observation by looking at generational trends. Generations that do not believe in their own merits accomplish more than generations preoccupied with merits. He writes:

> Over the past four decades, meritocratic elites have not governed very well. The elites who governed the United States from 1940 to 1980 were far more successful. They won World War II, helped rebuild Europe and Japan, strengthened the welfare state, dismantled segregation, and presided over four decades of economic growth that flowed to the rich and poor alike. By contrast, the elites who have governed since has brought us four decades of stagnant wages for most workers, inequalities of income and wealth not seen since the 1920s, the Iraq War, a nineteen-year, inconclusive war in Afghanistan, financial deregulation, the financial crisis of 2008, a decaying infrastructure, the highest incarceration rate in the

> world, and a system of campaign finance and gerrymandered congregational districts that makes a mockery of democracy.[23]

Generational data is difficult to interpret, and people will undoubtedly pick at Sandel's rhetoric, but the big picture is telling. From a theological point of view none of this is surprising. When we emphasize our merit, we tend to hoard, after all we worked for it. When we emphasize our indebtedness, good fortune, or grace, we tend to give.

Christ's love for us flows not because we were found worthy or possessed something meritorious. The naked truth of God's love for us is that it has very little to do with us. Our merits do not factor, which is good news considering that we have none. Does that mean that there are no merits at all? Here is where we need to appreciate an architectonic principle of scripture. The foundation of our salvation rests on the merits of Christ, not ours. Christ merited salvation for his people. He worked meticulously, perfectly, and infallibly. He was the faithful Adam, the perfect Israel, and the obedient son. He succeeded where all had failed.[24] So, God offers his people grace based on the meritorious work of his eternal and incarnate son. From this perspective, the fount of grace flows from the perfect work of Christ. This perspective gives us a new way of looking at work. It sets us free from the tyranny of merits so that we can actually work. Our labor becomes a joyful outflow of gratitude and love. To put it more sharply, we don't work to live, but we can live to work and share that fruit, a Copernican revolution of labor. If the work of another (Christ) benefitted us, then our work should benefit others. Work, therefore, is planted in a new kind of soil, not the kind that works to gain what is not gainable, but the fertile kind that works because it has gained what is not gainable for the benefit of all. [25] This work brings greater equality because it is rooted in the merits of another for others. Generosity begets generosity. And because those merits are efficacious, they will produce a harvest when we labor. And often that harvest is incommensurate with the work we put in.[26]

ENDNOTES

1. Sandel, *The Tyranny of Merit*, 74.
2. Sandel, *The Tyranny of Merit*, 74.
3. Longenecker, *Remember the Poor*, 25.
4. Sandel, *The Tyranny of Merit*, 14.
5. Delbanco, *College: What It Was, Is, and Should Be*, 138.
6. Young, *The Rise of the Meritocracy*, 103.
7. Young, *The Rise of the Meritocracy*, 120.
8. Acts 4:33.
9. Matt. 20:12.
10. Matt. 20:15.
11. Matt. 20:16.
12. Blomberg, *Interpreting Parables*, 224.
13. 2 Cor. 8:13.
14. 2 Cor. 8:10-12.
15. Tozer, *The Pursuit of God*, 27-38.
16. Marilynne Robinson insightfully points out that Abraham gave up two sons. Robinson, *Gilead*, 129.
17. Eckhart, *Selected Writings*, 47.
18. 2 Cor. 4:10. When we consider what Paul has given to other congregations, then no one outgave him. Hock writes: "Another cost that Paul had to absorb, if he wanted to keep his boast, was the personal cost. Tentmaking involved wearisome toil (6:5, 11:27); sleepless nights, hunger, and thirst (11:27); and in general, a life of having nothing, of being poor (6:10). Such is what Paul meant

when he said he would gladly spend and be physically spent for the sake of the Corinthians' soul (12:15)." Hock, *The Social Context of Paul's Ministry*, 64.

19. Phil. 1:4-6.

20. 1 John1:1-4.

21. Some manuscripts offer an alternate reading by changing the pronoun to ὑμῶν. See: Metzger, *A Textual Commentary on the Greek New Testament*, 639.

22. John 6:25-59.

23. Sandel, *The Tyranny of Merit*, 29.

24. For an excellent discussion on this topic, read Meredith Kline's *Kingdom Prologue*. This book is not for the faint of heart.

25. The sheer delight of work must not be overlooked as well. Concerning this point, Dorothy Sayers writes:

    "I have already, on a previous occasion, spoken at some length on the subject of Work and Vocation. What I urged then was a thoroughgoing revolution in our whole attitude to work. I asked that it should be looked upon, not as a necessary drudgery to be undergone for the purpose of making money, but as a way of life in which the nature of man should find its proper exercise and delight and so fulfill itself to the glory of God. That it should, in fact, be thought of as a creative activity undertaken for the love of the work itself; and that man, made in God's image, should make things, as God makes them, for the sake of doing well a thing that is well worth doing." Dorothy Sayers, *Letters to a Diminished Church: Passionate Arguments for the Relevance of Christian Doctrine*, 117.

26. Meredith Kline writes: "The eternal salvation of these individuals was, of course, a matter of divine mercy and grace through Christ.

But it pleased the Lord to invest their exemplary righteousness and outstanding act of covenantal devotion with special significance so that with reference to a typological manifestation of God's kingdom they prefigured Christ as one who received the kingdom of glory for the faithful performance of the messianic mission stipulated in his eternal covenant with the Father." Kline, *Har Magedon*, 79

"But now, since I no longer have any room for work in these regions, and since I have longed for many years to come to you, I hope to see you in passing as I go to Spain, and to be helped on my journey there by you, once I have enjoyed your company for a while. At present, however, I am going to Jerusalem bringing aid to the saints. For Macedonia and Achaia have been pleased to make some contribution for the poor among the saints at Jerusalem. For they were pleased to do it, and indeed they owe it to them. For if the Gentiles have come to share in their spiritual blessings, they ought also to be of service to them in material blessings. When therefore I have completed this and have delivered to them what has been collected, I will leave for Spain by way of you. I know that when I come to you, I will come in the fullness of the blessing of Christ. I appeal to you, brothers, by our Lord Jesus Christ and by the love of the Spirit, to strive together with me in your prayers to God on my behalf, that I may be delivered from the unbelievers in Judea, and that my service for Jerusalem may be acceptable to the saints, so that by God's will I may come to you with joy and be refreshed in your company. May the God of peace be with you all. Amen."

Romans 15:23-3

3

Generosity's Reconciling Power

No one disagrees that generosity is a beautiful thing. When we see it, it impresses us, such as when Warren Buffet pledged to give away 99% of his wealth to charities and other causes. When we see costly sacrifice mixed into it, it moves us even more such as when the widow with the two copper coins gave to the temple treasury in her poverty in Jesus's day or when the Macedonian churches begged to give to the work of God in their dire circumstances. Such generosity possesses the power to bridge deep divides and mend hostilities.

One of Paul's great desires was to bring reconciliation between Jews and Gentiles. However, he faced two challenges—one social, the other theological. From a social point of view, the Jews did not easily fit into the Greco-Roman world.[1] They were a small monotheistic group amidst a sea of polytheistic devotees. They tenaciously held onto their confession: The Lord our God, the Lord is one (*Kyrios ho theos, Kyrios heis estin*). Moreover, they had their own customs such as circumcision, dietary restrictions, and religious feasts and festivals. When we consider that religion touched every facet of life, the monotheism of the Jews and their practices separated them from the people of the Greco-Roman world. It is clear from Roman sources (Cicero, Suetonius, and Tacitus) that the Jews were an easily identifiable group, which shows there were social lines of demarcation.[2] These elements did not make them popular. In times of stress and social instability, public opinion could come down upon them. For example, the Jews were expelled from Rome under the emperors Tiberius and Claudius.[3] Leonard Rutgers, a classical archaeologist, offers a reasonable conclusion: "When law and order were maintained (in the eyes of Roman authorities), Jews had nothing to fear. When they were disturbed, as in 19 C.E. or under Claudius, legal and administrative measures were taken."[4]

Apart from these social markers, theological assumptions made them less inclined to interact with those around them. The Jews believed that they were God's chosen people. This idea was embedded in their stories from Abraham onward. Therefore, they knew they had a special position in God's dealing with humanity. Often this belief made them even more standoffish. From this theological perspective, the deepest divide in humanity is the one between Jews and Gentiles. God's goal of choosing the Jews, of course, was not to keep them apart from everyone else. Rather it was to bless the world through them. When the Jews were at their best, they mediated this blessing; when they were not, they placed boundary markers and excluded others by separating themselves. N. T. Wright makes this point: "[Israel] was determined to have her covenant membership demarcated by works of Torah, that is, by the things that kept that membership confined to Jews and Jews only..."[5]

Now comes Paul, and he desires to create unity between Jews and Gentiles after his radical conversion and new calling to bring the good news to Gentile communities. This is precisely why in several of his letters he addresses both groups and urges unity. To put it another way, he wants to bridge the greatest divide in humanity. How will he do so? On one level, he targets intellectual understanding. He offers a theology of grace. All are fallen, all are separated from God, and all are saved by grace.[6] Irrespective of original call, everyone is in the same boat. Therefore, no one can boast, not the Jew, not the Gentile. Paul also aims for the heart, and he does so through generosity. In his context, he sees an opportunity to show generosity and uses it to move toward reconciliation.

Economic hardships struck Judea and perhaps even a famine.[7] Life became difficult. At this point, Paul's heart went out to his people but instead of reaching out to a network of diaspora Jews to raise money, he did something counterintuitive. He reached out to the Gentile communities he established. Here we see the beginnings of something without parallel, a conviction that the church was a *transethnic* and *translocal* community with a worldwide vision.[8] If Paul could succeed, he would be a step closer to bringing together two groups. What is most surprising in all of this is that the struggling Macedonian churches were eager to give. Imagine the possible outcome of such giving. Paul goes to Jerusalem and meets the needs of Jewish believers at the expense of Gentile believers who are poorer than the ones in Jerusalem. Such generosity is unexpected, powerful, and moving—the very things that can bring reconciliation. Paul sees a disaster, a network of believers, a mission, and the power of generosity to bless the world. He had a few examples to follow.

In the book of Acts, a revival took place and God added converts daily, thousands of them. This fledgling community of believers did not return home. They lingered to hear more about Christ. Hence, the early church had to deal with infrastructural issues like food distribution. They created a system to give out food to those in need, particularly to widows. It was not a perfect system, and this point became apparent when Hellenistic Jews complained that their widows were being overlooked in Acts 6. The apostles deliberated, and they decided to commission the first set of deacons to take care of the logistics of doling out food. They commissioned seven men who were filled with the Spirit of God: Stephen, Philip, Procorus, Nicanor, Timon, Parmenas, and Nicolas.

A cursory glance at the names will reveal a commonality. All the names are Greek. The apostles only selected "deacons" from the very group that was being overlooked, the Hellenistic Jews. Moreover, the comment attached to Nicolas's name, "a convert to Judaism," sets the stage for future reconciliation between Jews and Gentiles. As early as Acts 6, we have a pattern—Gentiles blessing Jews. The early church saw a problem and addressed it with unexpected generosity. The outcome was reconciliation and growth. Paul wants the same for his churches.

Paul also knows that for change to happen, hearts need to be renovated. More specifically, the idea that the world is zero-sum must be shed. Paul also knows that only God can persuade people of this point, and often it is through the generosity of his people. Jesus's action of feeding the multitude furnishes an example.[9] When the crowds followed Jesus to hear him, they grew weary and hungry. His disciples, knowing this, asked him to send them away. They were most likely thinking of the elderly, infirm, and young. They could collapse on the way home if they stayed longer without sustenance. Jesus surprised his inner group by asking them to feed them with their meager provisions—five loaves and two fish. He used their act of giving to feed thousands and taught a spiritual principle—generosity and faith beget abundance, the opposite of zero-sum thinking. To emphasize this point, Matthew's gospel adds the detail that twelve basketfuls were left over.

What makes this interpretation even more powerful is that Jesus performed a second miracle of feeding the multitudes, but this time he does so among Gentiles. R. T. France, a New Testament scholar, points out that the feeding of the 4,000 took place within Jesus's ministry among Gentiles. In the preceding pericope, Jesus is in the region of Tyre and Sidon, and he heals a Canaanite woman's daughter. France, therefore, goes as far as to say, "[Matthew] 15:21-39 as a whole form a brief 'manifesto' for the extension of the Christian mission to the non-Jewish world."[10] Donald Hagner, another New Testament scholar, makes a similar point: "The feeding of the four thousand points to the blessing of the Gentiles, who, together with Israel, will also be the recipients of eschatological blessing through the provision of Jesus."[11] The seeds of global blessings are sown and in them lies the idea that generosity produces not only abundance but also the conditions needed for reconciliation to take place. Paul sees the power of generosity for reconciliation and pursues it.

In Romans 15:22-33, we see the aftermath of Paul's

appeal to the Corinthians. Because the churches in Macedonia and Achaea (where Corinth is situated) were pleased to donate to the poor in Jerusalem, we can conclude that Paul was successful in Corinth.[12] It was difficult, but the Corinthians gave to the work of God. What Paul says next is surprising. The Gentile churches owe it to the Jews to share their material possessions. The ESV's rendering captures the point: "For if the Gentiles have come to share in their spiritual blessing, they ought also to be of service to them in material blessing."[13] What Paul is saying is that there should be a mutuality when it comes to groups. Therefore, Paul urges both Jews and Gentiles to serve each other. Here is the point. If the church is going to be successful in its mission, reciprocity, generosity, and unity (which entails reconciliation) must be foundational. A reconciled people demonstrate the reality of God because only God can heal deep divisions and mend hostilities.

Paul also knows that when this mutuality exists, there will be blessing for all because people are created to be in community. In fact, if we turn our attention to the longest prayer of Christ in John's gospel, then the model of Christian community is the fellowship within the godhead—a pattern of giving and receiving. Hence, Jews and Gentiles ought to serve each other. And that extends to all groups then and now. However, this reciprocity is not a foregone conclusion. Paul knows this. He knows that it takes grace for people to give. He also knows that it takes grace for people to receive. This is why he asks the Romans to strive in prayer with him so that his collection for the Jerusalem church will be acceptable and well accepted.

Paul aims for one of the most important goals of humanity, reconciliation. Consider what he says in Galatians 3:28: "There is neither Jew nor Greek, there is neither slave nor free, there is no male and female, for you are all one in Christ Jesus." In one succinct verse, Paul lays out the three greatest divisions in humanity—racism, classism, and sexism, divisions that still exist today. The reason for this fact is not difficult to see. Technology, programs, laws, and the like help, but they do not get to the vitals of the issue. True change renovates hearts, reorients them, and sometimes resuscitates them. For these reasons, Paul's words to the Romans about the Jerusalem collection are important. They show us three key points.

First, Paul shows that generosity is the way forward. There will be no reconciliation, no community formation, and no lasting peace without it. A miserly community will never flourish; instead, it will bring further division and suspicion. Moreover, it will become provincial and inward. Jews will have Jewish communities and Gentiles will have Gentile communities. Groups will be siloed. In such a context, reconciliation will never take off the ground.

Only generosity has the power to overcome the deep divisions in society. Macedonian generosity can bless Judean hardships and create something beautiful.

Second, generosity provides the impetus to create reciprocity. When it does, then flourishing takes place. A small Hellenistic poem makes this point in an unexpected way. Theocritus, the ancient Syracusan poet, wrote bucolic poetry that captured the life of singing, herding, and enjoying the countryside. In "Idyll 8," two rustic figures, a cowherd (Daphnis) and a shepherd (Menaclas) decide to have a singing contest to pass the time. They set the prize (a nine-stop pipe) and enlist a nearby goatherd as the umpire. Then, they begin to sing. Each person sings four elegiac quatrains alternately and ends with two stanzas of hexameters. As readers work through the poem, they are pleasantly surprised that the shepherds bless each other. In the second set of quatrains, Menaclas sings:

> Ye woods and waters, wondrous race,
> Lith and listen of your grace;
> If e'vr my song was your delight
> Feed my lambs with all your might;
> And if Daphnis wend this way,
> make his calves as fat as they.[14]

Daphnis, not to be undone, in a contest of song, returns the good wishes.

Ye darling wells and meadows dear,
Sweet o' the earth, come lend an ear;
If like the nightingales I sing;
Give my cows good pasturing;
And if Menaclas e'ver you see,
fill his block and make him glee.[15]

The poem is charming, and as the poem progresses, a beautiful vision forms. In the end, the reader may realize that in a contest of reciprocal blessing, no one loses. Of course, one wins the prize (Daphnis has new pipes), but both poets win because the one who lost has been blessed better. When reciprocity is present, we will only have winners. That is the beauty of mutual generosity.

Someone will say that at best only one party will be generous. Probably true. But one party's generosity can create a cycle where the other responds in eventual generosity. Paul by bringing this collection to Jerusalem is praying for this reciprocity to take place. He knows that if he succeeds, the division between Jews and Gentiles can be bridged. Gentile generosity can lead to Jewish generosity.

Third, we need to be realistic because Paul is. It was challenging for him to get the Corinthians to open their hearts. And he knows that it will be challenging to get the church in Jerusalem to open their hearts as well. Paul knows that his mission may falter and fall, but not all falling is failure. In truth, all progress is filled with it. To put it another way, the point is not whether you will fall but whether you will fall backward or forward. From this perspective, there is only success in the work of reconciliation because it is always the way forward.

It is interesting to note that there is no further mention of what happened in Jerusalem. Did the Jerusalem church receive the finances favorably? What happened when Paul arrived? We will never know. Perhaps no outcome is given because what is important is not the outcome but the direction of the heart.

A decade ago, my congregation supported a farming project in a difficult country to operate. I wish I could say that the farm is thriving now; it is not. From one perspective, it was a failure, but from another perspective, it was an amazing success. This project allowed a family to stay in this difficult region, establish a church, locate a remote people group, and raise up people to serve them. The fruits are there, but the farm is not. Falling in the right direction by generosity is a beautiful fall, filled with grace. Where do we get the encouragement to take this step? Here we get to the heart of generosity. "For you know the grace of our Lord Jesus Christ, that though he was rich, yet for your sake he became poor, so that you by his poverty might become rich."[16] If we parse the logic, Christ's giving was completely one-sided. He did not give to people who reciprocated.

They were not worthy or even good. Yet, he still gave, and his consistent generosity toward them changed them (and us). That depth of divine generosity gives us a new way to live, a new logic of practice, and a new outlook. Moreover, to go back to the theme of this essay, it brings reconciliation between God and humanity.[17] And the good news is that reconciled people possess the wherewithal to bring further reconciliation to the world.

ENDNOTES

1. There were varieties of Judaism. Some Jews assimilated to their Hellenistic context. For example, Tiberius Julius Alexander was a Jewish procurator under the emperor Claudius. Later he was a Prefect of Egypt.
2. Williams, "The Expulsion of the Jews from Rome," 779.
3. Sources for Tiberius: Joseph., *Ant. Iud.* 18.81.4; Tac., *Ann.* 2.85.5; Seut., *Tib.* 36.1; Dio 57.18.5. Sources for Claudius: Acts 18:2; Suet., *Claud.* 25.4; Dio Cass. 60.6.6; Oros. 7.6.15.
4. Rutgers, "Roman Policy towards the Jews: Expulsions from the City of Rome during the First Century C.E," 74
5. Wright, *What Paul Really Said,* 130.
6. Rom. 1-3; Eph. 2:1-10.
7. Furnish, *II Corinthians,* 411. In 47, there was a famine in Judea. Acts 11:27-30; Joseph. *AJ* 20.51, 101.
8. Wright, *Paul, A Biography,* 94.
9. Matt. 14:13-21, Mark 6:31-44, Luke 9:10-17, John 6:1-14.
10. France, *Matthew,* 249.
11. Hagner, *Matthew 14-28,* 452.
12. Rom. 15:26-27.
13. Rom. 15:27.
14. Theoc. *Id.* 8.
15. Theoc. *Id.* 8.
16. 2 Cor. 8:9.
17. Rom. 5:9-11.

"But thanks be to God, who put into the heart of Titus the same earnest care I have for you. For he not only accepted our appeal, but being himself very earnest he is going to you of his own accord. With him we are sending the brother who is famous among all the churches for his preaching of the gospel. And not only that, but he has been appointed by the churches to travel with us as we carry out this act of grace that is being ministered by us, for the glory of the Lord himself and to show our good will. We take this course so that no one should blame us about this generous gift that is being administered by us, for we aim at what is honorable not only in the Lord's sight but also in the sight of man. And with them we are sending our brother whom we have often tested and found earnest in many matters, but who is now more earnest than ever because of his great confidence in you. As for Titus, he is my partner and fellow worker for your benefit. And as for our brothers, they are messengers of the churches, the glory of Christ. So give proof before the churches of your love and of our boasting about you to these men."

2 Corinthians 8:16-24

4

Triangulating Generosity

Who are the most generous? As a nation, America tops the charts.[1] The three most charitable cities in America are all in Idaho with an average giving rate of $17,977.[2] This means that major cities, where we might expect greater generosity, only have the perception of it. People in New York, Los Angeles, and Chicago give on average $3,308 per year. While we are on perception, those who live in Las Vegas, dubbed "Sin City," give three times more than New Yorkers.

In another study, the Barna Group found that age makes an enormous difference in giving. Eighty-four percent of millennials report giving less than $50 to charity per annum even though charitable giving ranks high on their priorities.[3] According to another source, households that make more than $75,000 are the least charitable. If we move to the church, then the average congregant gives 2.5 percent of his or her income annually. During the Great Depression, that number was 3.3 percent.[4] Thirty-seven percent of those who consider themselves evangelicals don't give at all to their churches. And when it comes to tithing only 2.7% do so.[5] If we look at the most religious group (top 20%), not based on beliefs but church membership, the statistics are more encouraging. This group gives 7% of their income.[6]

None of these statistics should surprise us. Recently, we had an election. The public wanted to see the tax returns of major candidates. Some courageously complied. And when they did, most Americans were disappointed because those who purport to be public servants give little. Kamala Harris has a giving rate of 1.3%, Bernie Sanders 3.4%, and Elizabeth Warren 5.5%. President Biden for the past twenty years hovered in the 1% range but ramped up towards elections.[7] Former President Trump still has not disclosed his tax returns. All of this is to say that we are not as generous as we think. In addition, we can't be too hard on the Corinthians. They are we.

The person who wrote the most well-known book on giving is Marcel Mauss, a French sociologist and the nephew of Émile Durkheim. In his book, *The Gift*, he explores how gift-giving works in society. His basic point is that giving demands reciprocal exchange, and this feature is foundational to society. From this perspective, the very act of giving can never be pure because the giver expects something in return, and the one who receives understands this point. Commenting on the practice of potlatch, which Mauss defines as the practice of gift giving in tribal societies, Mauss writes: "...the potlatch must be reciprocated with interest, as must indeed every gift."[8] This dynamic even extends to relationships in the family as well. Wives give to husbands expecting something in return and husbands give to their wives with the same expectation.[9] Mauss's point is that the practice of potlatch is still very much alive today in the modern world. So, invitations must be returned just as courtesies must, and "the round of drinks is every dearer and larger in size."[10] In a word, "we must give back more than we have received."[11] Giving, receiving, greater giving, obligation, and interest are all intertwined in this framework.

If we take a step back and reflect on the nature of giving, we are forced to say that Mauss has a point. It is easier to give to someone who will return that giving by twofold; threefold, even better. And it is easier to give to an organization that will recognize and honor you. Take away the incentives, the recognition, and the honors, and generosity will precipitously drop.

Paul knows the heart of people. He knows that giving is difficult and that pure giving is nearly impossible. So, he adds an important dimension, a vertical one. In the middle of 2 Corinthians 8, Paul says that he and his companions are administering the collection to honor the Lord himself.[12] The implication is that giving is not merely horizontal as if Gentile churches in Macedonia and Achaia are giving to Jewish ones in Jerusalem. Paul triangulates giving by adding God into the equation, and that makes all the difference. So, when someone gives, that person is primarily giving to the Lord and to people only secondarily. And within this framework, when someone receives, the logic is the same; that person is primarily receiving from the Lord and from people only secondarily.

One of the most noteworthy points about Paul's ministry is that he did not take finances from the churches he planted with one exception. This point is more remarkable because Paul says that the worker is worthy of his wages.[13] Furthermore, other teachers, such as traveling sophists, charged for their services, and a number of them became wealthy in the process. This dynamic dates to Plato and Xenophon (along with criticisms) and was in full swing in Paul's day where we see the beginning stages of what scholars call the Second Sophistic. Paul, therefore, could have relied on wealthy patrons for support or ask for payment, but he chose not to do so.[14] In other words, there were models available for Paul to follow, and he could have made a handsome and comfortable living.[15] That he did not follow any of these options begs for interpretation.

First, Paul did not want to vitiate his message. Some could have leveled the charge that he was preaching a new message for the pursuit of gain. His words to the Corinthians are clear as the midday sun: "For we are not, like so many, peddlers of God's word, but as men of sincerity, as commissioned by God, in the sight of God we speak in Christ."[16] His early mornings and late nights, working with leather as a tentmaker proves this point. He says to the Thessalonians that he worked with his own hands,[17] and to the Ephesians with whom he stayed for nearly three years, he says the same.[18] There is even some evidence that his hands might have been deformed on account of all the manual labor.[19] Second, Paul did not receive support from others because of the implications of a patron/client relationship.[20] By taking support, Paul would be under the direction and influence of a patron. David deSilva makes this point succinctly, "Grace [that is, favor] *must* answer grace, or else something beautiful will be defaced and turned into something ugly."[21] His point is that the kindness of a patron would have to be met with reciprocal kindness on Paul's part, which necessitates obligation. But Paul could not be in that situation because he was under God's direction alone. He needed to be free to follow Christ, especially as an apostle. Then why did he take finances from the Philippians?

Paul took finances from the Philippians for at least two reasons. He did so first because they insisted with tenacity. They even sent Epaphroditus to Paul when he was in prison, and Epaphroditus almost died on the way because of illness. Second, Paul and the Philippians had an understanding that they were in a partnership in ministry. This point comes out right in the beginning of the letter.[22] To put it another way, both the Philippians and Paul had the same mission from God. Most importantly, Paul knew that they understood that their giving was ultimately an offering to God. In other words, he received only what they gave to God. The most beautiful verse in the New Testament concerning giving is found in Paul's words to his beloved Macedonian church: "I have received full payment and have more than enough. I am amply supplied, now that I have received from Epaphroditus the gifts you sent. They are a fragrant offering, an acceptable sacrifice, pleasing to God."[23] If we could ask Paul who supplied all of his needs, he would say that God did, even if it was through Epaphroditus and the Philippians (for whom he is grateful). And if we could ask Paul who will bless the Philippians, he would give the same answer. "And my God will meet all your needs according to the riches of his glory in Christ Jesus."[24] The triangle is complete. The Philippians give to God, God gives to Paul, and Paul and the Philippians give to the world.

The profundity of Paul's words to his beloved church in Philippians 4:18 must not be lost—an acceptable and pleasing sacrifice to God. Giving was an act of worship on the church's part. So, when Paul received the gifts of the Philippians, it was a pure gift—no expectations, no strings, no sense of control, no binding obligations. What Marcel Mauss failed to see in his calculus of giving is this vertical dimension. When Christians at their best give, it is an offering to God. Because of this dimension, they can give purely, that is, anonymously (their left hand will not know what their right hand is doing, Matthew 6:3), they can give radically (they can live below their means, Luke 12:32-34), and they can give cheerfully (2 Corinthians 9:6-7). Mauss is right in one sense. Without a divine angle, we can only give to influence and receive. The ancient adage, *do ut des* (I give so that you might give) is the logic of the world.

One of the privileges of being a pastor is getting to know people. In all my churches, there were always one or two people who exemplified giving in an amazing way. The first time I experienced this was when I started my first church. It consisted predominantly of college students, and yet we were always self-sufficient without outside support. To this day, I don't know how it worked.

One day, I received a call from the parent of a student. She was kind and explained that her daughter wrote a large check to the church. She politely asked if that money could be returned. I said that I would inquire because I never looked at the giving, a practice that served me well over the years. The treasurer over the finances confirmed the donation, and we were ready to give this money back. As we were about to return her money, the student halted it. She persuaded her parents that her giving was noble and good. To this day, I do not know how much that money was, but it was generous, sacrificial, and most importantly godward, a fragrant aroma to God. This student who gave did not want special privileges, acknowledgement, or praise. In a few years, she left, as all students do. Her giving was pure because she was not giving to the church, or to a minister, or to anyone else. She was giving to the God who gave himself for her. Can giving be pure? Yes, but only when giving to others is first giving to God.

If we go back to the text, there is also a horizontal element. Paul wants to show the integrity of his giving. At least three times, Paul mentions those who will be involved. Titus, a trusted man, will accompany Paul.[25] Paul also says that Titus will accompany "the brother who is praised by all the churches for his service to the gospel."[26] Unfortunately, Paul does not mention who this person is by name, but his reputation will go a long way to safeguard against any hint of impropriety. Finally, Paul mentions another unnamed person who is described as proven and zealous.[27] This triumvirate, along with Paul, will transport the funds to the church in Jerusalem.

We don't have to wonder why Paul is giving all these details because he writes: "For we are taking pains to do what is right, not only in the eyes of the Lord but also in the eyes of man."[28] Paul's dealings with finances are pellucid. Paul knows that with finances integrity is paramount. The accusation of impropriety, greed, venality, and the like could cripple his work. So, he takes optics into consideration. Maturity and love always do.

There is a lesson for the church today. We would do well to ask what the world thinks about it. Does the world think that the church is a body that loves to bless people at its own expense, or does it think that the church is a body that wants to enrich itself at the expense of others? Does the world think that the church is characterized by great generosity or by a great love of money? Does the world think that the church is transparent in its giving or veiled in its greed? Optics matter, especially in an age of social media. I pray that when the world looks at the church that it sees a giving and generous body, one willing to give its cloak, to walk the extra mile, and to turn the other cheek. It would behoove us to think about the church's reputation.

None of this will be easy, but if we are going to be a body that blesses, brings healing, and steps toward reconciliation, then the vertical and horizontal dimensions of giving must be firmly rooted in practice. But how? Here the vertical and horizontal elements come into play in the heart of the Christian message. The father gives his son, the son gives his life on the cross, the father and son send the Holy Spirit, and the Holy Spirit gives comfort, guidance, and power. From this movement, we can say that God gives. We can also say that Christians receive. In fact, the definition of a Christian is one who receives—forgiveness, adoption, the sealing of the Spirit—in reality, every blessing in the heavenly realms.[29] And so, because Christians have received and because the source of divine blessings is inexhaustible, they can give. The completion of receiving is giving, and this creates a cycle because the one who gives is more blessed than the one who receives.

If anyone can give purely, then it is the Christian. And this pure giving is what the world needs to see and experience. In that movement, it will see flashes of God's heart of generosity for the world.

ENDNOTES

1. Radu, Sintia. "Which Countries Are the Most Generous?" *U.S. News & World Report,* December 19, 2019. https://www.usnews.com/news/best-countries/articles/2019-12-20/the-worlds-most-generous-countries.

2. "The 10 Cities Where the Most GENEROUS Practicing Christians Live." Barna Group. Accessed February 14, 2021. https://www.barna.com/research/generous-pcs/.

3. "Generations & Generosity: How Age Affects Giving." Barna Group. Accessed February 14, 2021. https://www.barna.com/research/generations-generosity-age-affects-giving/.

4. "Church and Religious Charitable Giving Statistics." Nonprofits Source. Accessed February 14, 2021. https://nonprofitssource.com/online-giving-statistics/church-giving/.

5. Smith and Davidson, *The Paradox of Generosity,* 100.

6. Haidt, *The Righteous Mind,* 308.

7. Light, Joe, Laura Davison, and Bloomberg. "How Much Money Democratic 2020 Candidates Gave to Charity in 2018." *Fortune,* April 26, 2019. https://fortune.com/2019/04/26/2020-democratic-candidates-charity/.

8. Mauss, *The Gift,* 53.

9. Mauss, *The Gift,* X.

10. Mauss, *The Gift,* 65.

11. Mauss, *The Gift,* 65.

12. 2 Cor. 8:19.

13. 1 Tim. 5:18.

14. Bruce Winter writes: "It can be appreciated with what ease the 'politics of the secular associations and civic life could be replicated by the heads of leading Christian households in the Christiaan 'meeting' (ἐκκλησία). Winter, *After Paul Left Corinth*, 191.
15. Hock, *Social Context of Paul's Ministry*, 52-59.
16. 2 Cor. 2:17.
17. 2 Thess. 3:8. Other references include: 1 Thess. 2:9; Acts 18:3, 20:34; 1 Cor. 4:12; 2 Cor. 12:14.
18. Acts 20:34.
19. Hock, *Social Context of Paul's Ministry*, 14.
20. deSilva, *Honor, Patrongage, Kinship & Purity*, 95-119.
21. deSilva, *Honor, Patrongage, Kinship & Purity*, 109.
22. Phil. 1:5.
23. Phil. 4:18.
24. Phil. 4:19.
25. 2 Cor. 8:16.
26. 2 Cor. 8:18.
27. 2 Cor. 8:22.
28. 2 Cor. 8:21.
29. Eph. 1:3.

"The point is this: whoever sows sparingly will also reap sparingly, and whoever sows bountifully will also reap bountifully. Each one must give as he has decided in his heart, not reluctantly or under compulsion, for God loves a cheerful giver. And God is able to make all grace abound to you, so that having all sufficiency in all things at all times, you may abound in every good work. As it is written,

'He has distributed freely, he has given to the poor;
his righteousness endures forever.'

He who supplies seed to the sower and bread for food will supply and multiply your seed for sowing and increase the harvest of your righteousness. You will be enriched in every way to be generous in every way, which through us will produce thanksgiving to God. For the ministry of this service is not only supplying the needs of the saints but is also overflowing in many thanksgivings to God. By their approval of this service, they will glorify God because of your submission that comes from your confession of the gospel of Christ, and the generosity of your contribution for them and for all others, while they long for you and pray for you, because of the surpassing grace of God upon you. Thanks be to God for his inexpressible gift!"

2 Corinthians 9:6-15

5

Dying and Reaping

When my son was in second grade, his teacher had the class plant beans in Styrofoam cups. All the students could see at first was topsoil. I could imagine them wondering if something would really grow. A day passed, nothing. Another day and still the same. But in time, the students began to see a shoot of green, peeking through the soil. After a few weeks, the students saw the miracle of life.

My son proudly gave his plant to his grandmother. She took this plant and cared for it. That was over a decade ago. That single plant has produced more than a decade of beans. When I visit my parents, the story of the bean plant somehow always emerges. And during the summers, my daughter, a decade younger than my son, harvests the beans with my mother.

Seeds are amazing. They look lifeless, they are small, and they seem so insignificant, but they contain the potential of life. God created this pattern, and it forms the basis of a spiritual principle. We see it in Jesus's parable when he speaks of a mustard seed. The mustard seed might be the smallest of seeds, but it becomes the largest garden plant. The growth of seeds is inevitable, explosive, and exponential. And if we theologize this point, then the mustard seed, a symbol of God's kingdom, grows to bless the world. Paul taps into this principle and reminds the Corinthians to sow. However, before they do so, they need to understand two points. First, sowing needs to be generous. Second, God sows in them; their sowing is in response to his.

There comes a point in the life of an organization when people begin to wonder what it is all about. One reason for this is that there is little growth and no harvest. A farmer, who toils and sees nothing, will question farming. In time, frustration will bring an end to labors. Churches can fall into this pattern of "harvestlessness" because they fail to sow generously. Paul makes this point clear. If the Corinthians sow sparingly, they will reap sparingly, but if they sow generously, they will reap generously. The key words to underline are the adverbs. Paul wants the Corinthians to experience a harvest, and there is only one way it will take place.

Let's imagine what kind of harvest the Corinthians will have in their sowing. Paul offers some clues. He says people would overflow in many expressions of thanksgiving and praise God.[1] This outcome is remarkable. Corinthian generosity can cause people nearly two thousand miles away to burst into thanksgiving and praise to

God. There is something about generosity that moves people like few things can.

One of the goals, if not the main goal of Christianity, is to reach people with the love of Christ. Christians call it the Great Commission (based on the words of Jesus in Matthew 28:16-20). For the Great Commission to become a reality, people need to incline their hearts to God in faith. This entails no longer living for themselves, stepping away from idols (inordinate and disordered desires), and living for the one who has given his life for them.[2] We are talking about a fundamental change in a person's life. Who can change people? What can change them? If we take Paul's words seriously, then generosity can.

Most would agree that the main idol of the world is money. What makes New York, London, Seoul, and other cities move is Mammon. He causes us to go to bed late at night and wake up early in the morning. So, when we see the opposite, sowing generously, that is, giving away resources on account of love, it moves us. And God uses that generosity to change a person's vision and eventually that person's heart. Generosity shows that there is something more important in this world. By giving up and giving away what others deem most important, we show the preciousness of the love of Christ.

Two decades ago, there was an article in a publication called *The Voice of the Martyrs*. It recounted the brutal persecution of Christians in North Korea. Granted that information is difficult to obtain in a closed country, history proves we should not discount or disbelieve in stories of human depravity and grave suffering. Often these stories prove to be true in hindsight; we only need to think about the atrocities in the Soviet Union in the 1930s, The Great Leap Forward of the CCP in 1950s and 1960s, and the brutal regime of Khmer Rouge in the 1970s.[3]

While the government was burrowing underground to build a subway, officials hit upon an underground church. The government ordered the members of the church to recant their faith. The officials threatened them with death and the hanging of their children if they did not do so. These North Korean Christians would not recant, something unfathomable to people living in the West. As nooses were placed around their children's emaciated necks, parents said to them with amazing faith and love that they would see them shortly in heaven. The children were executed. Next, a steamroller revving its engine in the background was heard. The officials gave another opportunity to the church to recant. The church refused. Mothers, fathers, brothers, and sisters lay there in the dirt and began singing a hymn as the steamroller came their way.

In this story, we see a sowing of the greatest kind. The sowing of lives. These Christians gave what was most important. When people in North Korea come to understand that kind of generous sowing, they will see Christ's love because it underlines the ultimate sacrifice of Christ. Moreover, that sowing will produce a harvest because God does not forget the blood of his children.[4] In a word, the greater the sowing, the greater the vision of God's grace, and the greater the harvest. It all begins with sowing seeds.

The life of David Brainerd shows this point in a similar way. The fruitfulness of David Brainerd was underground when tuberculosis cut his life short. He lived from 1717-1747 when the First Great Awakening was thundering through the colonies. He attended Yale College for two years before getting expelled for saying that a tutor in the college (Chauncey Whittelsey) had "no more grace than a chair." Brainerd confessed to making this comment and wrote a letter of apology, but the decision of Thomas Clap (the rector) and the trustees remained firm.[5] Thereafter, Brainerd toiled among the Native Americans in New York, Pennsylvania, and New Jersey for four years before his death. In the process, he suffered tremendously. Physically, he was ill-suited to a life in the wilderness. According to his journal, he was coughing up blood even while he was studying at Yale.[6] In the wilderness, his sufferings compounded. He also traveled more than 3,000 miles on horseback and foot in his four-year labor.[7] Temperamentally, he suffered from depression, which made his work more difficult. Brainerd's only visible success was in Crossweeksung, New Jersey, where he established a small congregation but left when he sensed that he was dying. [8] He was right; shortly thereafter he died in the home of Jonathan Edwards. In view of these points, Norman Pettit has argued that Brainerd was a failed missionary and one unsuited for the field.[9]

David Brainerd could not have imagined what kind of impact he would have. His journal entries, which were reluctantly published posthumously, and Edwards's work on his life made an impact that can still be felt around the world. It would not be an exaggeration to say that his life was the single greatest catalyst for the modern missionary movement. The picture of Brainerd in the wilderness, toiling, praying, and suffering captured the hearts of millions.

John Wesley prepared an abridgment of Edwards's longer work, *The Life of David Brainerd,* and used it to inspire Methodist circuit riders.[10] Countless missionaries took a copy of *The Life of David Brainerd* on the field, people like Levi Parsons, the first American missionary to Palestine and Pliny Fisk, an early missionary to Egypt. When Fisk was seriously ill in Egypt, he wrote in his journal: "What must not Brainerd have suffered, when sick among the Indians?"[11] He, too, died as a young man on the field at the age of 33. Others who found inspiration in Brainerd's life include giants in the history of the modern missionary movement: William Carey, Andrew Fuller, John Ryland, Henry Martyn, Robert M'Cheyne, David Livingstone, and Andrew Murray.

Apart from these missionaries, his life became the seed for major institutions that still exist today. He inspired Eleazar Wheelock to start a school for Indians and colonists (1748), which eventually became Dartmouth College.[12] Brainerd even made a small donation to the school upon selling his tea kettle and pot, which amounted to four pounds.[13] Francis Asbury, the influential fourth president of Brown University, enthusiastically testified to Brainerd's influence.[14] And in an unforeseen turn of events, Brainerd helped form The College of New Jersey (Princeton University) because of the ill-treatment he received at Yale. Presbyterians in New Jersey and New York were displeased with how Yale treated him. Jonathan Dickinson and Aaron Burr, the first and second presidents of the college not only knew Brainerd but cared for him in his sickness. At one point Brainerd was convalescing at Dickinson's home while classes for the college had just begun in his living room. He also officiated over Dickinson's wedding.[15]

From one perspective, we may say with Pettit that Brainerd was a failed missionary, but from another perspective, one that looks beyond the life of a person, we can say that his life was a seed that was sown. And only when his body was buried deep in the earth, did it produce a harvest. At this juncture, we need to confront an irresistible aspect of sowing. Sowing entails a type of dying. Jesus said it best when he reminded his disciples that a seed must die before it produces a harvest.[16] Only by dying do we see the broader picture, namely that it will produce a harvest that is greater than our giving.

Now we come to the other truth of sowing, namely that God is the ultimate sower. At least three times, Paul mentions that God is the one who pours grace upon the Corinthians. In 2 Corinthians 9:8, Paul reminds the Corinthians that God is able to bless them abundantly so that they can abound in every good work. In 2 Corinthians 9:10, Paul writes that God is the one who supplies seeds to the sower so that there will be an enlarged harvest. In 2 Corinthians 9:14, Paul makes mention of the surpassing grace of God which God has given to the Corinthians. The Corinthians can sow because God has sown his grace in them. Two key points come to the fore.

First, we give because we have been given. God never asks us to give something that we have not already received in abundance through his grace. The logic is cogent. God calls us to forgive others because we have been forgiven. Likewise, we extend patience because God has been patient with us. And we love the unlovable because God loved us when we were dead in our sins and transgressions. So, we give generously because God has been generous with us. From this perspective, we are only giving what we have received.

Second, Paul reminds the Corinthians that when they give, God will bless them. Here are his words: "And God is able to make all grace abound to you, so that having all sufficiency in all things at all times, you may abound in every good work."[17] Some people take this to mean that when we give, the harvest will be health and wealth for us. The problem with this interpretation is that it is too narrow, too materialistic, and too consumeristic. In other words, our sowing will lead to great blessings, but those blessings do not always have a monetary value because no amount of money can equal the abundance God gives. For example, when we give generously, one of the greatest blessings that God bestows is the freedom from the love of money and the shedding of our selfishness. Only when we overcome these twin vices can we enjoy life, which is priceless.

In the New Testament book of James, the author rails against the wealthy who oppress the poor. They do so because they love and serve wealth. Selfishness, if left unchecked, will always cripple by maiming the legs of joy from running. In this context, James says to the rich that their fine clothes are already moth-eaten, and their gold and silver are already corroded.[18] James's point is that selfishness destroys all enjoyment in the present and the future. It is like buying a very expensive pair of shoes. They are so perfect and precious that you rarely wear them. So, you don't wear them, which cancel their very function. And when you do wear them, you are so worried that you are going to stain them that you can't enjoy the outing, the company, and the moment. At that point, not only are your shoes moth-eaten but so is your life, just like the rich man who builds bigger barns only to die that very night.[19] By sowing generously, God frees you and allows you truly to live.

God can also bless monetarily. The health and wealth gospel is not entirely wrong. The logic of sowing demands a harvest. And this harvest does not always have to be spiritualized. There are many stories of generous people whom God has blessed so that they can give more. To put this point on firmer footing, let's examine the broad sweep of the modern missionary movement.

If we survey the history of the modern missionary movement, nations that possessed fervor for world missions have grown in wealth and influence—England, the United States of America, South Korea, Singapore, and Brazil, to name a few. Let me focus on South Korea. In 1953, South Korea was one of the poorest countries in the world. Its GDP was below $100 per capita. Now it is one of the wealthiest countries with a GDP of over $40,000 per capita.[20] What makes this rapid prosperity even greater is that the nation lacks natural resources. How did this development happen?

There is no doubt that scholars will give many reasons for South Korea's assent. But it is interesting to note that the rise of Korea's economy has kept in pace with its missionary fervor. The church wanted to reach the world and God honored their sowing (prayers, passion, and willingness to bless the nations) by raising the country so that it could reach the world. For example, South Korea has no oil, but it refines the oil of petroleum rich countries, and Korea's microchips, electronics, and cars are in every corner of the world, not to mention its music, drama, food, and fashion. All these avenues open doors for the sharing of Christ's love.[21] Today, the only country that sends more missionaries than South Korea is America,[22] and that gap is closing. According to Joel Kim, the president of Westminster Seminary in California, in 2017 South Korea sent 27,436 missionaries.[23]

At this point, a caveat is in order. The rise of nations is not without problems and complications. With God's blessings and abundance, there will be those who desire to use it for self-serving ends. History proves this point time and again, and we are seeing some of that now. God's grace always comes with a risk. People can use it to bless others at their expense or enrich themselves at the expense of others.

If we look at things from a sociological perspective, there is compelling evidence that religion and economics are strongly tied together. In 2010, Peter Berger wrote an article whose title (in all capital letters) summarizes his main point, "MAX WEBER IS ALIVE AND WELL, AND LIVING IN GUATEMALA: THE PROTESTANT ETHIC TODAY."[24] As one can see, Berger's article is a revisitation and reapplication of Weber's thesis. Berger argues where Pentecostalism flourishes, the economy rises because Pentecostalism possesses "this-worldly asceticism," by which he means a disciplined attitude toward work (not just hard work), a disciplined attitude towards various spheres of social life (notably the family), a deferral of instant consumption, and a strong emphasis on the importance of education. He finds evidence of this kind of Pentecostalism in Guatemala, Brazil, and sub-Saharan Africa. More pertinent for this essay, he sees economic flourishing. Berger's point is straightforward: Weber was right to conclude that religion and economics share a *Wahlverwandshaft*, that is, an affinity.[25]

So, what does all of this mean for us? First, we should pray for a heart that loves to sow for the simple reason that God loves a cheerful giver.[26] Second, we should take stock of all the gifts and resources that God has deposited and begin to dream about sowing. Third, we should take steps of faith and sow generously. There will be uncertainties, risks, and variables, but none of these things should hinder sowing. Remember that Paul did not know how his collection would be received by the churches in Jerusalem, yet he took a step of faith. God, in his perfect timing, will bring forth that harvest. In the meantime, we sow and that generously. And we can find encouragement to do so because at the heart of our faith rests the greatest sowing that has ever taken place. To use the words of Matthew, Jesus spent three days and nights in the heart of the earth only to rise again.[27] That sowing has given birth to cosmic restoration and life.

ENDNOTES

1. 2 Cor. 8:12-13.
2. Idol worship in the modern world is usually on account of disordered loves, a point that Augustine made long ago in his work, *Doctr. Chr.* 1.27-28, and *De Civ.* 15.22. For the best modern treatment on idols, see Tim Keller's *Counterfeit Gods*. "A counterfeit god is anything so central and essential to your life that, should you lose it, your life would feel hardly worth living." Keller, *Counterfeit Gods*, xviii.
3. Evans, Stephen. "Remembering North Korea's Christian Martyrs." *BBC News*. December 26, 2016. https://www.bbc.com/news/world-asia-38404012. In addition, Fyodor Dostoevsky's *Brothers Karamazov* offers penetrating insight into human depravity, especially book 5.
4. Rev. 6:9-11.
5. Pettit, "Prelude to Mission: Brainerd's Expulsion from Yale," 37. Pettit offers Brainerd's full letter of apology.
6. Edwards, *The Life of David Brainerd*, 146.
7. Edwards, *The Life of David Brainerd*, 2.
8. Edwards, *The Life of David Brainerd*, 298-428.
9. Edwards, *The Life of David Brainerd*, 3.
10. Conforti, "David Brainerd and the Nineteenth Century Missionary Movement," 316.
11. Conforti, "Jonathan Edwards's Most Popular Work: 'The Life of David Brainerd' and Nineteenth Century Evangelical Culture," 198.
12. Wheelock. *A Plain and Faithful Narrative of the Original Design,*

Rise, Progress, and Present State of Indian Charity-school at Lebanon, in Connecticut, Gale ECCO, 2010.

13. Edwards, *The Life of David Brainerd,* 583.
14. Conforti, "David Brainerd and the Nineteenth Century Missionary Movement," 309.
15. Edwards, *The Life of David Brainerd,* 441.
16. John 12:24.
17. 2 Cor. 9:8.
18. James 5:2-3. James uses the perfect tense in Greek. The future has broken into the present. πλοῦτος ὑμῶν σέσηπεν καὶ τὰ ἱμάτια ὑμῶν σητόβρωτα γέγονεν, ὁ χρυσὸς ὑμῶν καὶ ὁ ἄργυρος κατίωται καὶ ὁ ἰὸς αὐτῶν εἰς μαρτύριον ὑμῖν ἔσται καὶ φάγεται τὰς σάρκας ὑμῶν ὡς πῦρ. ἐθησαυρίσατε ἐν ἐσχάταις ἡμέραις.
19. Lk. 12:16-21.
20. PricewaterhouseCoopers. "The World in 2050." PwC. Accessed March 14, 2021. https://www.pwc.com/gx/en/research-insights/economy/the-world-in-2050.html.
21. N. T. Wright states: "The mission of the church is the reality of which the pagan empire is the parody." Wright, *What Paul Really Said,* 148.
22. Onishi, Norimitsu. "Korean Missionaries Carrying Word TO HARD-TO-SWAY PLACES." *The New York Times,* November 1, 2004. https://www.nytimes.com/2004/11/01/world/asia/korean-missionaries-carrying-word-to-hardtosway-places.html.
23. Challies, Tim. "Which Country Sends the [Second] Most Missionaries?" Tim Challies, February 21, 2018. https://www.challies.com/articles/which-country-sends-the-second-most-missionaries/.

24. Berger, "MAX WEBER IS ALIVE AND WELL, AND LIVING IN GUATEMALA: THE PROTESTANT ETHIC TODAY." Also see Gifford and Nogueria-Godsey, "The Protestant Ethic and African Pentecostalism: A Case Study."

25. Berger, "MAX WEBER IS ALIVE AND WELL, AND LIVING IN GUATEMALA: THE PROTESTANT ETHIC TODAY," 8.

26. 2 Cor. 9:7.

27. Matt. 12:40.

"For I am already being poured out as a drink offering, and the time of my departure has come. I have fought the good fight, I have finished the race, I have kept the faith. Henceforth there is laid up for me the crown of righteousness, which the Lord, the righteous judge, will award to me on that day, and not only to me but also to all who have loved his appearing. Do your best to come to me soon. For Demas, in love with this present world, has deserted me and gone to Thessalonica. Crescens has gone to Galatia, Titus to Dalmatia. Luke alone is with me. Get Mark and bring him with you, for he is very useful to me for ministry. Tychicus I have sent to Ephesus. When you come, bring the cloak that I left with Carpus at Troas, also the books, and above all the parchments. Alexander the coppersmith did me great harm; the Lord will repay him according to his deeds. Beware of him yourself, for he strongly opposed our message. At my first defense no one came to stand by me, but all deserted me. May it not be charged against them! But the Lord stood by me and strengthened me, so that through me the message might be fully proclaimed and all the Gentiles might hear it. So I was rescued from the lion's mouth. The Lord will rescue me from every evil deed and bring me safely into his heavenly kingdom. To him be the glory forever and ever. Amen."

2 Timothy 4:6-18

6

What Paul Gave

Up to this point, we have focused on Paul's theology of generosity. Now it is time to ask the question: What did Paul give? One way to answer this question is by looking at the beginning, middle, and end of his ministry. Such a panoramic sweep will allow us to see his development.

When it comes to the beginning of Paul's ministry, Acts 9 is a good place to begin. There we see a young zealot, who sought to be faithful to God, even by means of violence, a veritable hardliner who believed actions spoke louder than words. This point should not surprise us in view of the stories of zeal that Paul grew up hearing, such as the story of Phinehas and his slaying of a couple in the context of idolatry and immorality and the zeal of Elijah that challenged and cut down the priest of Baal.[1] N. T. Wright reminds us: "...for the modern Christian 'zeal' is something you do on your knees, or in evangelism, or in works of charity; for the first-century Jew 'zeal' was something you did with a knife."[2] Until his conversion and call, Paul approved of the stoning of Stephen.[3]

We read about the details of his calling through Ananias when God bids him to go to Paul to minister to him. Ananias is understandably apprehensive. He points out Paul's past record of persecution and his present intention to continue. God responds to Ananias: "Go, for he is a chosen instrument of mine to carry my name before the Gentiles and kings and the children of Israel. For I will show him how much he must suffer for the sake of my name."[4] At this point, the reader does not know what will befall Paul or what he will do, but two points about his calling are clear. As a chosen instrument, he will bear witness to Gentiles and suffer much. From that moment, the pattern of Paul's calling is set.

When we come to the middle of Paul's ministry, after his third missionary journey, we see him in Troas (Troy) in Acts 20. There he does something without explanation. He sends his companions ahead by ship while he walks from Troas to Assos.[5] During this time, the Holy Spirit warns him of the dangers that lie ahead in Jerusalem. What makes these dangers even more real is the rioting that already has taken place in Ephesus and his past record of suffering—stoning, floggings, imprisonment, and psychological torment.[6] Paul is fully aware that his life hangs by a few threads. He says as much to the Ephesian elders who come to see him on the shores of Troas in Acts 20:22-25:

> And now, behold, I am going to Jerusalem, constrained by the Spirit, not knowing what will happen to me there, except that the Holy Spirit testifies to me in every city that imprisonment and afflictions await me. But I do not account my life of any value nor as precious to myself, if only I may finish my course and the ministry that I received from the Lord Jesus, to testify to the gospel of the grace of God. And now, behold, I know that none of you among whom I have gone about proclaiming the kingdom will see my face again.

The apostle does not know the details of the future, but he knows that difficulties lie ahead, and yet he sets his face like flint to meet them.[7]

In the very next chapter, on three occasions, faithful disciples aim to deter Paul from going to Jerusalem. At Tyre, Paul stays with fellow believers for seven days. During that time, they tell him not to go on to Jerusalem. The tense of the verb changes to the imperfect, which connotes continual action,[8] suggesting that the disciples repeatedly tell him not to go. The author of Acts even adds the detail that the disciples spoke through the Holy Spirit.[9] A few verses later, we find Paul in Caesarea at the house of Philip, the evangelist. There a prophet named Agabus arrives and enacts a symbolic action. He takes

Paul's belt and binds his own hands and feet and says: "This is how the Jews at Jerusalem will bind the man who owns this belt and deliver him into the hands of the Gentiles."[10] This is the second time that Agabus has appeared in the book of Acts. In Acts 11:28, he prophesied that there would be a famine. That the famine took place during the reign of the emperor Claudius lends gravity to his predictions. The emphasis on suffering is perspicuous. Therefore, it is not surprising that those with Paul urge him not to proceed to Jerusalem. By the end of the passage, Paul is still undeterred.

Is Paul being stubborn by not listening to the prophets? Is he flouting the words of the Holy Spirit? Has not God warned him no less than three times not to go to Jerusalem? Most scholars interpret this passage as brotherly concern for Paul, not divine directive, forbidding him to enter Jerusalem. For example, C. K. Barrett argues that the words of this chapter are not as clear as they could be. In other words, Paul was not disobeying prophecy because the prophets were only stating that suffering awaited. More importantly, their dissuading him from Jerusalem was borne out of their love and concern for him.[11] Hans Conzelmann agrees: "'Through the Spirit' does not imply that Paul is now commanded not to go to Jerusalem. The warning arises from the concern of those to whom the Spirit unveils the future."[12] Other scholars, like Devin White, view Paul from a philosophical perspective and argue that he was weighing prophecy from a rational point of view. He writes: "Paul's recognition of two competing oracles provides an opportunity for Luke to strengthen his characterization of Paul as a pious, courageous, and rational figure who is capable of both honoring and evaluating divine messages."[13]

When we examine Paul's actions in light of his calling, we do not need to resort to hermeneutical gymnastics. Right from the beginning, Paul knows that his calling is to be a witness and to suffer for Christ's name. So, when the Holy Spirit warns that suffering is waiting for him in Jerusalem, he embraces it; he is stepping deeper into his calling.

Here is where the detail that Paul walked from Troas to Assos becomes significant. By the time he is at Troas, he knows that suffering on account of his message and mission is near (Acts 20:22-25). Therefore, it is reasonable to believe that he needs time alone to wrestle with the words that affliction and imprisonment await him. So, his journey on foot[14] is used to process, pray, and perhaps even plead. If Paul took Roman roads, the journey would have been 31 miles, a two-day trip. It was his Gethsemane, his wrestling with God to say, "not my will but yours be done." Moreover, his journey uncannily maps onto the pattern of Jesus's passion, which includes a farewell address, a trip to

Jerusalem, suffering, and testifying before public officials. When Paul is reunited with his companions, he resolves to move into Jerusalem with firmness, like his Lord, stepping with equal steps into the footprints he left.

If we zoom out, starting from Acts 21 to the end, we see an acceleration in Paul's calling to witness and suffer. He preaches to his fellow Jews in Jerusalem in Acts 21-22, the Jewish council in Acts 23, Felix and Festus, Roman procurators in Acts 24-25, King Agrippa in Acts 26, and the inhabitants of the island of Malta in Acts 28. During that time, he suffers an arrest, an assassination attempt, an imprisonment, and a shipwreck. If the tradition of the church is correct, he suffers martyrdom under the Emperor Nero.

In Paul's decision to head to Jerusalem, we see an uncompromising soul, one who is committed to laying hold of his calling. The language that Paul uses in Philippians 3:12 underlines this point; his words are economical, powerful, and purposeful. He writes: "I pursue so as to take up that for which I was taken by Christ Jesus."[15] In a word, Paul aims to embrace his call.

When we come to the last letter of Paul, we see a picture of faithfulness, especially as we connect his language from 2 Timothy 4:6-8 to the book of Philippians. In both letters, Paul uses an evocative verb in the passive voice. He says that he is being poured out like a drink offering (*spendomai*).[16] Such wording jars both modern and ancient readers. For modern readers living in the West, the idea of a libation is foreign, and it might connote wastefulness—when something is poured out, it is no more. For ancient readers, the imagery is common but only when the verb is in the active voice. In other words, people do the pouring to honor some deity. Therefore, it is interesting to note that Paul makes the verb passive.[17] Paul is not pouring out a libation; he is the libation that is being poured out.

The books of Philippians and 2 Timothy are also connected by the use of a small Greek adverb, *ādā*, which means "already." We can hear the echo of one passage in the other. In Philippians 3:12, Paul says that he has *not already* attained his calling, and in 2 Timothy 4:6, he says that he *is already* poured out. In other words, in Philippians, he is a man in the midst of his ministry striving to fulfill his calling, and in 2 Timothy he is a man who has stayed the course and is now contemplating his death. The athletic imagery in both books makes the same point. In Philippians, he is pressing and straining; in 2 Timothy, he is finishing and ending. In addition, great pathos fills this passage. He is alone (he tells Timothy to come to him quickly), he has been betrayed (Demas deserted him, and Alexander did him much harm), and he is cold (he asks for his cloak), and he is waiting to give the last drops of his libation-life to his Lord, who is ever present with him. The cumulative effect of his language points to martyrdom.[18]

There are many things we can say about the whole of Paul's life. We can say that he was faithful to his calling, obedient to his Lord, and determined with his mission. All these perspectives are correct, but we can add another. We can say that he was magnanimous. He loved God and he loved people, and this love manifested in a generous spirit that endured all hardships from sleepless nights to martyrdom for people. So, we come back to the question with which we started this essay: What did Paul give?

Everything.

ENDNOTES

1. Num. 25; 1 Kings 18.
2. Wright, *What Paul Really Said*, 27.
3. Acts 9:1.
4. Acts 9:15.
5. Acts 20:13.
6. For an insightful summary on the suffering of Paul, see N. T. Wright, *Paul—A Biography*, 235-337.
7. It is also tempting to see a broader movement westward, like Aeneas before him in Vergil's epic. Both men travel from Troy and land upon the Italian peninsula to establish a kingdom, one earthly, the other heavenly. I owe this insight to Louis Markos.
8. ἔλεγον, Acts 21:4.
9. διὰ τοῦ πνεύματος, Acts 21:4.
10. Acts 21:11.
11. Barrett, *Acts-Volume II*, 990.
12. Conzelmann, *Acts of the Apostle*, 178.
13. White, "Confronting Oracular Contradiction in Acts 21:1-14," 46.
14. πεζεύω can be translated as "travel on foot." Acts 20:13.
15. ...διώκω δὲ εἰ καὶ καταλάβω, ἐφ' ᾧ καὶ κατελήμφθην ὑπὸ Χριστοῦ ['Ιησοῦ]. Notice the use of the active and passive of the same verb.
16. 2 Tim. 4:6 and Phil. 2:17.
17. BDAG, s.v. "σπένδω."
18. Diebelius and Conzelmann, *The Pastoral Epistles*, 121.

"After these things the word of the Lord came to Abram in a vision: 'Fear not, Abram, I am your shield; your reward shall be very great.' But Abram said, 'O Lord God, what will you give me, for I continue childless, and the heir of my house is Eliezer of Damascus?' And Abram said, 'Behold, you have given me no offspring, and a member of my household will be my heir.' And behold, the word of the Lord came to him: 'This man shall not be your heir; your very own son shall be your heir.' And he brought him outside and said, 'Look toward heaven, and number the stars, if you are able to number them.' Then he said to him, 'So shall your offspring be.' And he believed the Lord, and he counted it to him as righteousness."

Genesis 15:1-6

7

Imagination and Generosity

If you are like me, then you probably never heard a lecture, presentation, or sermon about imagination. As an educator, I've been thinking about the importance of imagination for a few years, after reading C. S. Lewis's short book, *The Abolition of Man*, where writes: "The task of the modern educator is not to cut down jungles, but to irrigate deserts."[1] The work of irrigation entails engaging and watering imaginations. In this process, I've come to three conclusions.

First, the world speaks about the importance of imagination more than the church. John Lennon and Yoko Ono's song "Imagine" is an example. It has topped all charts. It is a song with a dreamlike quality in which Lennon and Ono imagine a utopian world without boundaries, without religions, and without countries. The assumption is that boundaries are the cause for conflict. If only we could remove them. The lyrics long for an end to wars and strife and for the establishment of peace.

Lennon sings and asks his listeners to imagine with him. The chorus says:

> You may say I'm a dreamer
> But I'm not the only one
> I hope someday you'll join us
> And the world will be as one.

When Lennon says that he is not the only one, he is right. He has touched millions of people if not hundreds of millions. And they, too, long for peace, and they see boundaries as impediments to a better world. The intentions are noble.

Hollywood is the epicenter of tapping into our imaginations. It casts a vision for people to reimagine the world. Every movie has a message, and if the movie is crafted well, that message lingers and seeps into our imaginations and shapes us. The sitcom, *Friends,* captured a generation of young people to move into New York City and *The Matrix* did more to popularize Jean Baudrillard's nearly unreadable book on simulation and simulacra by a thousand percent![2] There is an important point here. Propositional truths, pure reason, sustained argumentation, and the like do not primarily move people. We are much more complex beings, not just heads. Particularly in our age, reason does not stand a chance against our hearts. What moves us is our passions, and behind our passions sit our imaginations.

The second conclusion is that imagination is the most powerful force in the world. This statement might sound hyperbolic, but the evidence is around us. Consider Elon Musk. One day he decided to create an electric car to impact the world. He believed that Tesla would be better than every other manufacturer. He is a game-changer. Now he desires to explore space, and his company SpaceX is rivaling national programs. What is his secret? Musk will tell you that the two keys to his success are taking risks and his imagination.[3] Musk imagines something, and he labors to make it a reality.

Another example comes from a novel by Lawrence Thornton, *Imagining Argentina*.[4] The protagonist, Carlos Ruenda, discovers that he has a gift. He can imagine the fate of those who have been abducted by the military regime of Argentina (1976-1983). As mothers and fathers of missing children hear about his gift, they flock to his home, and in his backyard garden he shares what he sees. The uncanny accuracy of his imaginings persuades even the most skeptical. When his wife, Cecelia, and daughter, Teresa, are taken, he frantically searches for them. At one point in the novel, he surmises that it is his imagination that keeps his wife alive. The book does not confirm whether his thought is correct, but it offers an important insight: our imaginations create the world.

Consider that what we see around us was once only in a person's mind. I look out the window of my school, and I see a building complex. Before this twenty-story brick structure went up, someone imagined it. Then this person, perhaps in a committee, made a case for it to be built on the Upper West Side of Manhattan. Three playgrounds dot the building. Before they were built, someone imagined children running, playing, and hanging on the jungle gym. If I walk out of my building and head east, I step into a community garden, which is beginning to burst into the brilliant colors of spring—fiery red petals, emerald-green leaves, and canary-yellow bulbs. Someone imagined this garden as well. All of this is to say that the first step of creating comes from our imaginations. Then we speak and build. The gospel of John makes a similar point. In the beginning was the word, the word was with God, and the word was God, and all things came into being through that word. In short, God imagined the world and spoke it into existence.

At this point, a brief caveat is necessary. Imagination does not always produce beauty. In fact, if you do a search for the word "imagination" in the Bible, most instances are negative.[5] The picture that emerges is one of people following their evil inclinations through their imaginations. For example, Psalm 73:7 says: "From their calloused hearts comes iniquity; their evil imaginations have no limits" (NIV). Isaiah 65:2 says the same thing. "All day long I have held out my hands to an obstinate people, who walk in ways not good, pursuing their own imaginations" (NIV). The problem here is that people's imaginations are not tethered to God's word but to their own sinful desires. Here is the point. Our imaginations need a starting point, a soil in which to germinate, take root, and grow. That starting point or that fertile soil must be God. This leads me to my third conclusion.

The starting point of our imaginations makes all the difference. If the grounding of our imagination is sinful, then creative sinfulness will emerge. If the grounding of our imagination is goodness, truth, and beauty, namely God himself, then creative goodness, creative truth, and creative beauty will surface. Imagination works best when it binds itself to God. G. K. Chesterton made this point when he said: "Those who leave the tradition of truth do not escape into something which we call freedom. They only escape into something else, which we call fashion."[6] I would add that fashions go out of style, or as Peter Berger once wrote (recalling the words of W. R. Inge, the dean of St. Paul's Cathedral): "He who marries the spirit of the age soon finds himself a widower."[7] Abraham, the patriarch, offers a different paradigm.

God approaches Abram in Genesis 15 in a vision and reconfirms his promises to him. It is significant that

God comes to him at this point because Abram had just engaged in combat with several kings to rescue his nephew, Lot. Not only was Abram's life in jeopardy (a reprisal was almost certain), but he also was wondering whether he would ever have a son. These are the very themes that God reminds him of. God says: "Fear not, Abram, I am your shield; your reward shall be very great."[8] Immediately, Abram points out what is uppermost in his mind, namely that he is childless. Here God promises him that he will have a child and through that child many other descendants. "Look toward heaven, and number the stars, if you are able to number them…So shall your offspring be."[9]

God touched Abram's imagination. The text, then, says that Abram believed. That was the turning point of his life, what gave his life shape and direction. God allowed him to use his physical eyes to see an invisible reality and make that invisible reality into a vision worth pursuing. This is what Paul calls faith:

> In hope he believed against hope, that he should become the father of many nations, as he had been told, "So shall your offspring be." He did not weaken in faith when he considered his own body, which was as good as dead (since he was about a hundred years old), or when he considered the barrenness of Sarah's womb. No unbelief made

> him waver concerning the promise of God, but he grew strong in his faith as he gave glory to God, fully convinced that God was able to do what he had promised. That is why his faith was "counted to him as righteousness" (Rom. 4:18-21).

Abraham believed and walked in faith because his imagination, tethered to God's promises, fired his heart.

If this reading is correct, imagination, touched by God's word, strengthens faith. And faith exercised strengthens imagination. Imagination, therefore, gives spiritual eyes, the ability to see what is not there, and the power to birth it into existence. Therefore, we neglect our imaginations to our peril, a point about which Walter Bruggeman, the great Old Testament professor, warns the church.

Brueggemann reminds us that cultivating our imaginations will not be easy. He grounds his arguments in Israel's history. At one point, Israel lost its ability to imagine. It started during the reign of Israel's kings. The kings created an intellectual and social milieu that domesticated people and even temple worship. And under Solomon, Israel became Canaanized.[10] The people, therefore, could only see what royal power wanted them to see, which Brueggemann calls royal consciousness. Other options became invisible, unthinkable, and even untruthful. Incrementally, Solomon re-enslaved his people. According to 1 Kings 5:13-15, he conscripted thirty thousand men for his building projects. He also had seventy thousand carriers and eighty thousand stonecutters. Finally, exile came, and the lack of imagination continued.[11] Israel replaced their kings for others.

This is why the prophets are so important. They see the world through different eyes. In a word, they can imagine. Brueggemann writes: "It is the vocation of the prophet to keep alive the ministry of imagination, to keep on conjuring and proposing future alternatives to the single one the king wants to urge as the only thinkable one."[12] The goal, therefore, is to imagine a better world, one that is different from the agenda set forth by the hegemonic forces that be: Hollywood, Silicon Valley, New York, Washington, Beijing, Moscow, and Berlin. And it is to do so in a way that "cannot be readily coopted or domesticated by hegemonic interpretive power."[13] The vision of the world is strong, but the irony is that that vision constricts and blinds rather than gives sight. The author of Deuteronomy was right: "...and you shall grope at noonday, as the blind grope in darkness."[14] Isaiah was also right: "We grope for the wall like the blind; we grope like those who have no eyes; we stumble at noon as in the twilight, among those in full vigor we are like dead men."[15]

The church must be an alternate voice, must offer

an alternate vision, and must live an alternate life, one between heaven and earth. It must bring down heaven and lift earth heavenward. So, how can it accomplish these feats? If we take our cues from the prophets, then we need to lose our lives in God's story. Let me borrow an illustration from N. T. Wright. In one of his articles, he speaks of a Shakespearean play.[16] He asks his readers to imagine the discovery of a new play, a veritable masterpiece, but there is one problem. The play is missing the fifth act. What can be done? He suggests that we allow experienced Shakespearean actors to drink in the play and make it their own. And when the final act comes, they improvise. They use their imaginations, which is tethered to the play and the Shakespearean corpus. We should do the same as believers. We should imbibe the word of God, meditate on the character of God, and grow in the experience of the Holy Spirit, and reimagine the world. Then, like Abraham and Paul, walk out in faith to do, to serve, to build, and to love. If believers lived this kind of life, we would undoubtedly bring beauty down from heaven and plant it on earth where it will grow.

Here is the amazing part of it. God asks us to give our imaginations over to him. To put it more pointedly, the spirit of prophecy is upon his people because the Spirit of God dwells with his people. We are prophets in Christ and have a prophetic mantle if we care to receive it. If we tie this thought to generosity, the theme of these essays, then we can have generous imaginations and imaginative generosity, the very things we need to bless the world.

ENDNOTES

1. Lewis, *Abolition of Man,* 13-14.
2. Baudrillard's *Simulation and Simulacra* is a difficult book to understand but worth the read.
3. Evannex. "Tesla and SpaceX CEO Elon Musk's Vivid Imagination Results in Huge Risks." *InsideEVs,* February 3, 2018. https://insideevs.com/news/335886/tesla-and-spacex-ceo-elon-musks-vivid-imagination-results-in-huge-risks/.
4. Thornton, *Imagining Argentina,* 1991.
5. Ps. 73:7; Isa. 65:2; Ezek. 13:2; Ezek. 13:17.
6. Chesterton, *The Well and the Shallows,* 57.
7. Berger, *The Adventures of an Accidental Sociologist,* 75.
8. Gen. 15:1.
9. Gen. 15:5.
10. Brueggemann, *The Prophetic Imagination,* 24.
11. Brueggemann argues that the church today, like Israel, is in exile. Brueggemann, *Hopeful Imagination,* 93.
12. Brueggemann, *The Prophetic Imagination,* 40.
13. Brueggemann, *The Prophetic Imagination,* XXVI.
14. Deut. 28:29.
15. Isa. 59.10.
16. Wright, "How Can the Bible Be Authoritative," 7-32.

8

Conclusion

When the pandemic started, I started a book club with a handful of people from around the country. The wonders of Zoom. We have been meeting for over a year now. We plowed through a host of authors from Camus to Barfield to Hume to Niebuhr to MacIntyre. I benefited greatly from these conversations, and I have made new friends.

When we first read David Hume, I vehemently disagreed with his ethics. I could not believe that he wrote the following words: "Reason is, and ought only to be the slave of the passions, and can never pretend to any other office than to serve and obey them."[1] The idea that our rationality was a slave to our passions struck me as simply wrong. And when Hume stated that it *ought to be* a slave to our passions, I found that statement wrong and dangerous. I asked myself where his foundation of morality was. I did not have to wonder long. He makes it clear where he locates morality—in our sentiments. He writes:

> You never can find it, till you turn your reflection into your own breast, and find a sentiment

> of disapprobation, which arises in you, towards this action. Here is a matter of fact; but 'tis the object of feeling, not of reason. So that when you pronounce any action or character to be vicious, you mean nothing, but that from the constitution of your nature you have a feeling or sentiment of blame from the contemplation of it.[2]

In this context, Hume is saying that what causes people to avoid vices is a feeling in their guts.[3] You just know that it is wrong to kick a puppy, steal from a neighbor, or hurt another person. I agreed to a certain point, but how can something so fickle as our feelings or sentiments be the basis for our morality? Moreover, people's sentiments change all the time, not to mention that different people have different sentiments.

I also thought to myself that Hume, unbeknownst to himself, could make such a remark because he was living under the auspices of Scottish Presbyterianism. In other words, the sentiments of most around him were uniform enough because of the legacy of the Kirk. Few doubted the importance of oath keeping, industry, and the lawfulness of private property. In addition, MacIntyre's words that the Enlightenment was one of the most self-unaware periods lingered in my mind. Yet, I still admired Hume's courage. So, I decided to read a biography about his friendship with Adam Smith by Dennis Rasmussen, *The Infidel and the Professor: David Hume, Adam Smith, and the Friendship that Shaped Modern Thought.*

Once I picked up the book, it was difficult to put down. Not only is Rasmussen an excellent writer, but the friendship between Hume and Smith was beautiful to see. Here is one quote that encapsulates their friendship:

> The earliest of the letters open with a formal "Dear Sir," but it was not long before they transitioned to the more affectionate "Dear Smith" or "My Dear Hume," then "My Dear Friend," and finally, "My Dearest Friend"—an epithet that neither of them used with any other correspondent during the course of their friendship.[4]

Later both men would say that friendship was the chief joy of life. Also, Rasmussen's side comments were insightful windows into the eighteenth century, such as when Hume was denied a professorship at Edinburgh University in moral philosophy because he could not uphold the Westminster Confession of Faith. Rasmussen painted a picture of Hume that was lovable. Hume was consistent, honest, jolly, hospitable, self-deprecating, and courageous. I began to like him more. My mind still disagreed with his moral philosophy, but my heart warmed to him. Fast forward eight months. I picked up Jonathan

Haidt's book, *The Righteous Mind,* and there I found Hume once again.

I was certain that Haidt was going to say that Hume's views on morality were wrong, but I was mistaken. In the first third of the book, Haidt makes a case for a Humean understanding of morality. He uses an illustration of a rider and an elephant to make his point. The rider represents controlled processes and rationality, the elephant automatic ones, including emotions, intuitions, and passions.[5] Haidt argues that in the relationship between the two, the elephant takes the lead, and the rider follows. And often the rider functions as a press secretary. Haidt writes: "Reasoning can take us to almost any conclusion we want to reach, because we ask, 'Can I believe it?' when we want to believe something, but 'Must I believe it?' when we don't want to believe. The answer is almost always yes to the first question and no to the second."[6] I thought these words were insightful and more importantly true to life.

Midway through the book, I could see the world through Hume's eyes—our sentiments lead the way, and our rationality follows. I examined my own life, and I had to admit that Hume and Haidt had a point. When I was in college, there was a minister whom I admired. His sermons were eloquent, powerful, and cogent. A year later, as I began to read more theological material, I realized that many of this man's sermons were plagiarized verbatim, even the illustrations. I could not believe it. At that point, my sentiments towards him soured, an indication of my petty self-righteousness, which I am embarrassed to admit. Even though he did not say anything that I disagreed with, my mind would try to find fault. In the reverse, there were some ministers I loved. When they said something that was questionable, I saw the best in it. My mind would even create elaborate stories to see these ministers in the best possible light. All of this is to say my mind followed my heart; the elephant led the way and my mind functioned as a press secretary—very Humean of me!

My wife and I love to host people at our apartment. We often invite people who would not ordinarily meet. Theologically, philosophically, culturally, and socially, they are from different worlds. One benefit of such dinners is that people get to know each other. Many have become friends, and they have grown fond of each other. Why? Their elephants moved or in the least began to lean. Riders, therefore, began to rationalize why someone in a different camp was a pretty good person. I could see before my eyes the truth of Haidt's point. If we add generosity into the framework, then we can see why it is so powerful. To riff off Haidt's language, generosity speaks to elephants.

From a theological perspective, Haidt's insight corresponds to a biblical worldview in three ways. First, sin affects hearts and minds. One is not more or less fallen than the other. When it comes to the fallenness of the mind, theologians call it the noetic effects of sin (*nous* in Greek means mind). Hence, to focus only on the mind is to forget that the mind is fallen. A better approach is to aim for the heart and mind together. Generosity reaches the heart and gives room and time for the head to consider and reconsider, a point that Haidt makes as well. Even two minutes of pause or reflection can open elephants to counsel.[7] What we need is time with people—the more, the better. Second, in a broken world, especially in our age where our emotions rule, controversies and debates are interminable.[8] Therefore, we do not get very far through reason alone. In fact, there is no rational basis for morality in a postmodern world. If, therefore, we are going to make progress, generosity must play a key role because it reaches hearts. It forges bonds and creates connections. Finally, because there is a logic of which the mind does not know, an intangible and invisible force that tugs at hearts, we must not lose sight of things that reach the depths of a person. In chapter 10 of the Westminster Confession of Faith, there is a chapter on Effectual Calling. It reads:

> This effectual call is of God's free and special grace alone, not from anything at all foreseen in man, who is altogether passive therein, until, being quickened and renewed by the Holy Spirit, he is thereby enabled to answer this call, and to embrace the grace offered and conveyed in it.

Consider the wording: free, special grace, not foreseen in man, quickened, enabled, and renewed. All these words underline something that God does in his people. It is his generosity touching the inward parts. In a very real way, we have been transformed by God's generosity. Therefore, our generosity, too, by God's grace, can reach the hearts of others. It is a way forward.

ENDNOTES

1. Hume, *A Treatise on Human Nature,* 266.
2. Hume, *A Treatise on Human Nature,* 301.
3. Adam Smith developed Hume's ideas further in *A Theory of Moral Sentiments.*
4. Rasmussen, *The Infidel and the Professor,* 4.
5. Haidt, *The Righteous Mind,* 53.
6. Haidt, *The Righteous Mind,* 107.
7. Haidt, *The Righteous Mind,* 79-82.
8. MacIntyre calls this philosophic outlook emotivism. See: MacIntyre, *After Virtue,* 6-22.

Postscript

Before the book went to print, I drove to Princeton with my family. Princeton has the blessing of having very old trees, the kind that cicadas love. As soon as we left the main highway, all we could hear was the sound of cicadas. At the suggestion of my wife, we listen to Bob Dylan's song, "Day of the Locusts." Dylan wrote this song when he was awarded an honorary degree (Doctor of Music) from Princeton University in 1970. The day was hot, and tensions were high over the Vietnam War. As people were giving speeches, the singing of cicadas overwhelmed everything and everyone. Amplification systems have nothing on a billion cicadas singing in unison. Dylan was glad to leave. He sings:

> I put down my robe, picked up my diploma
> Took hold of my sweetheart and away we did drive
> Straight for the hills, the black hills of Dakota
> Sure was glad to get out of there alive.

Leave he did. That was fifty-one years ago, three sets of seventeen years. It appears that cicadas know prime numbers. Two points worth considering. First, cycles exist. Second, the song of a billion can overwhelm any voice, no matter how powerful. I hope that we learn to sing a new song. And if it starts with incomprehensible droning, so be it.

Bibliography

Barrett, C. K. *Acts—Volume II*. London: T & T Clark,1998.

Baudrillard, Jean. *Simulation and Simulacra*. Ann Arbor, University of Michigan Press, 1994.

Bauer, Walter, William F. Arndt, and F. Wilbur Gingrich. *Greek-English Lexicon of the New Testament and Other Early Christian Literature*. Chicago: University of Chicago Press, 1957.

Berger, Peter L. "MAX WEBER IS ALIVE AND WELL, AND LIVING IN GUATEMALA: THE PROTESTANT ETHIC TODAY," *The Review of Faith & International Affairs*, 8.4, (2010): 3-9, DOI: 10.1080/15570274.2010.528964

_____. *The Adventures of an Accidental Sociologist*. New York: Prometheus Books, 2001.

Blomberg, Craig. *Interpreting the Parables*. Downers Grove, InterVarsity, 1990.

Brown, Peter. *Poverty and Leadership in the Later Roman Empire*. Hanover: Brandeis University Press, 2001.

Brueggemann, Walter. *Hopeful Imagination—Prophetic Voices in Exile*. Minneapolis: Fortress Press, 1986.

_____. *The Prophetic Imagination*. Minneapolis: Fortress Press, 2018.

Büchler, Adolph. *The Economic Conditions of Judea After the Destruction of the Second Temple*. London: Jewish College Publications, 1912.

Chadwick, Henry. *The Early Church*. New York: Penguin, 1993.

Challies, Tim. "Which Country Sends the [Second] Most Missionaries?" Tim Challies, February 21, 2018. https://www.challies.com/articles/which-country-sends-the-second-most-missionaries/.

Chesterton, G. K. *The Well and the Shallows*. San Francisco, Ignatius Press, 2006.

"Church and Religious Charitable Giving Statistics." Nonprofits Source. Accessed February 14, 2021. https://nonprofitssource.com/online-giving-statistics/church-giving/.

Conforti, Joseph. "David Brainerd and the Nineteenth Century Missionary Movement." *Journal of the Early Republic* 5, no. 3 (1985): 309-29.

______. "Jonathan Edwards's Most Popular Work: "The Life of David Brainerd" and Nineteenth-Century Evangelical Culture." *Church History* 54, no. 2 (1985): 188-201.

Conzelmann, Hans. *Act of the Apostles*. Philadelphia: Fortress, 1987.

Delbanco, Andrew. *College—What It Was, Is, and Should Be*. Princeton: Princeton University Press, 2014.

DeSilva, David A. *Honor, Patronage, Kinship & Purity*, Downers Grove: IVP, 2000.

Dibelius, Martin and Conzelemann, Hans. *The Pastoral Epistles*. Philadelphia: Fortress, 1972.

Eckhart, Meister. *Selected Writings*. Translated by Oliver Davies. New York: Penguin, 1994.

Edmonds, John Maxwell. *The Greek Bucolic Poets*. Cambridge: Harvard University Press, 2007.

Edwards, Jonathan. *The Life of David Brainerd*. Edited by Norman Pettit. New Haven: Yale University Press, 1985.

Elliot, J. K. *The Apocryphal New Testament*. Oxford: Clarendon, 1993.

Evans, Stephen. "Remembering North Korea's Christian Martyrs." *BBC News*. December 26, 2016. https://www.bbc.com/news/world-asia-38404012.

Evannex. "Tesla and SpaceX CEO Elon Musk's Vivid Imagination Results in Huge Risks." InsideEVs. InsideEVs, February 3, 2018. https://insideevs.com/news/335886/tesla-and-spacex-ceo-elon-musks-vivid-imagination-results-in-huge-risks/.

France, R. T. *Matthew*. Grand Rapids: Eerdmans, 1997.

Furnish, Victor Paul. *II Corinthians*. New Haven: Yale University Press, 2008.

Gates, Charles. *Ancient Cities—The Archaeology of Urban Life in the Ancient Near East and Egypt, Greece, and Rome*. New York: Routledge, 2011.

"Generations & Generosity: How Age Affects Giving." Barna Group. Accessed February 14, 2021. https://www.barna.com/research/generations-generosity-age-affects-giving/.

Gifford, Paul, and Trad Nogueira-Godsey. "The Protestant Ethic and African Pentecostalism: A Case Study." *Journal for the Study of Religion* 24, no. 1 (2011): 5-22.

Hagner, Donald. *Matthew 14-28*. Grand Rapids: Thomas Nelson, 2000.

Haidt, Jonathan. *The Righteous Mind*. New York: Vintage Press, 2012.

Harris, Paul. "David Brainerd and the Indians: Cultural Interaction and Protestant Missionary Ideology." *American Presbyterians* 72, no. 1 (1994): 1-9.

Harris, Murray. *2 Corinthians*. Grand Rapids: Eerdmans, 2005.

Hock, Ronald. *The Social Context of Paul's Ministry*. Minneapolis: Fortress, 2007.

Hume, David. *A Treaties on Human Nature–Volume 1*. Oxford: Clarendon Press, 2007.

Jiménez, Jesus. "Billions (Yes, Billions) of Cicadas Soon to Emerge from Underground." The *New York Times*, March 28, 2021. https://www.nytimes.com/2021/03/28/us/cicada-brood-x.html.

Keller, Timothy. *Counterfeit Gods*. New York: Penguin, 2009.

"Korean man under probe for attacking Japanese woman in Seoul." *Korea Times*. (2019, August 25). https://www.koreatimes.co.kr/www/nation/2019/08/251_274485.html.

Klein, Ezra. *Why We're Polarized*. New York: Avid Reader Press, 2020.

Kline, Meredith. *Har Magedon*. Eugene: Wipf & Stock, 2006.

______. *Kingdom Prologue*. Eugene: Wipf & Stock, 2006.

Lewis, C. S. *The Abolition of Man*, New York: HarperOne, 2001.

Light, Joe, Laura Davison, and Bloomberg. "How Much Money Democratic 2020 Candidates Gave to Charity in 2018." *Fortune*, April 26, 2019. https://fortune.com/2019/04/26/2020-democratic-candidates-charity/.

Longenecker, Bruce. *Remember the Poor*. Grand Rapids: Eerdmans, 2010.

Maalouf, Amin. *In the Name of Identity—Violence and the Need to Belong*. New York: Penguin, 2000.

MacIntyre, Alasdair. *After Virtue*. Notre Dame: Norte Dame University Press, 1984.

MacMullen, Ramsey. *Roman Social Relations*. New Haven: Yale University Press, 1974.

Mauss, Marcel. *The Gift: The Form and Reason for Exchange in Archaic Society*. New York: Routledge, 1990.

Meeks, Wayne. *Origins of Christian Morality*. New Haven: Yale University Press, 1993.

Metzger, Bruce. *A Textual Commentary on the Greek New Testament*. Stuttgart: Deutsche Bibelgesellschaft, 1994.

Nock, Arthur Darby. "Religious Attitudes of the Ancient Greeks." *Proceedings of the American Philosophical Society*, 85.5 (1942): 472-482.

O'Brien, Peter T. *The Epistle to the Philippians*. Grand Rapids: Eerdmans, 1991.

Onishi, Norimitsu. "Korean Missionaries Carrying Word TO HARD-TO-SWAY PLACES." *The New York Times*, November 1, 2004. https://www.nytimes.com/2004/11/01/world/asia/korean-missionaries-carrying-word-to-hardtosway-places.html.

Pettit, Norman."Prelude to Mission: Brainerd's Expulsion from Yale." *The New England Quarterly* 59, no. 1 (1986): 28-50.

Postman, Neil. *Technopoly*. New York: Vintage Books, 1993.

Radu, Sintia. "Which Countries Are the Most Generous?" *U.S. News & World Report*, December 19, 2019. https://www.usnews.com/news/best-countries/articles/2019-12-20/the-worlds-most-generous-countries.

Rasmussen, Dennis C. *The Infidel and the Professor*. Princeton: Princeton University Press, 2017.

Robinson, Marilynne. *Gilead*. New York: Picador, 2004.

Rutgers, Leonard Victor. "Roman Policy towards the Jews: Expulsions from the City of Rome during the First Century C.E." *Antiquity*, 13.1 (1994): 56-74.

Sandel, Michael. *The Tyranny of Merit: What's Become of the Common Good?* New York: Farrar, Straus and Giroux, 2020.

Sayers, Dorothy. *Letters to a Diminished Church: Passionate Arguments for the Relevance of Christian Doctrine.* Nashville: Thomas Nelson, 2004.

Smith, Christian & Davidson, Hilary. *The Paradox of Generosity.* Oxford: Oxford University Press, 2014.

Stark, Rodney. *The Rise of Christianity.* New York: Harper Collins, 1997.

Tarn, W. W. *Hellenistic Civilization.* New York: Meridian Books, 1952.

"The 10 Cities Where the Most GENEROUS Practicing Christians Live." Barna Group. Accessed February 14, 2021. https://www.barna.com/research/generous-pcs/.

Thiselton, Anthony. *The First Epistle to the Corinthians.* Grand Rapids, Eerdmans, 2000.

Thornton, Lawrence. *Imagining Argentina.* New York: Bantam Books, 1991.

Tozer, A. W. *The Pursuit of God.* Chicago: Moody Bible Institute, 2006.

White, Devin L. "Confronting Oracular Contradiction in Acts 21:1-14." *Novum Testamentum,* 58.1 (2016): 27-46.

Winter, Bruce. *After Paul Left Corinth.* Grand Rapids: Eerdmans, 2001.

Wright, N. T. "How Can the Bible be Authoritative?" *Vox Evangelica* 21, (1991): 7-32.

______. *Paul—A Biography*. New York: HarperOne, 2018.

______. *What Paul Really Said*. Grand Rapids: Eerdmans, 1997.

Veyne, Paul. *Bread and Circuses: Historical Sociology and Political Pluralism*. New York: Penguin, 1990.

Wheelock, Eleazer. *A plain and faithful narrative: of the original design, rise, progress and present state of the Indian charity-school at Lebanon, in Connecticut*. Hansebooks, 2014. Kindle.

Williams, Margaret H. "The Expulsion of the Jews from Rome in A.D. 19." *Latomus* 48, no. 4 (1998): 765-784.

Young, Michael. *The Rise of the Meritocracy*. Middlesex: Penguin, 1961.

About the Author

John Lee is an educator and a minister in the Christian Reformed Church. He has taught at various institutions and currently serves at the Geneva School of Manhattan. He obtained his M.A., M.Phil., and Ph.D. in history from Yale University. His essays have appeared in *The Banner*, *Christianity Today*, and several other publications. He lives in New York City and East Hampton with his wife and two children.